BORDEN
His Life and World

JOHN ENGLISH

BORDEN

His Life and World

General Editor: W. Kaye Lamb

Picture Editor: Paul Russell

McGraw-Hill Ryerson Limited

Toronto Montreal New York London

ISBN 0-07-082303-0

1 2 3 4 5 6 7 8 9 10 BP 6 5 4 3 2 1 0 9 8 7

Printed and bound in Canada

Canadian Cataloguing in Publication Data

English, John, 1945—
  Borden

(Prime Ministers of Canada)

Bibliography: p.
Includes index.
ISBN 0-07-082303-0

1. Borden, Robert Laird, Sir, 1854-1937. 2. Prime ministers — Canada —
Biography. 3. Canada — Politics and government — 1911-1921.* I. Series.

FC556.B76E54   971.06'12'0924   C77-001514-X
F1033.B76E54

Contents

Preface

"This war is the suicide of civilization," Robert Borden, Prime Minister of Canada, wrote in his diary in the spring of 1915 when the first news of Canadians killed in France reached home. Three years later, the war ended; civilization had survived; but the wounds to civilization and to Canada were profound and debilitating. In the aftermath of war, Canadians harked back to the days before August 1914, to what seemed a brighter adolescent moment of national life. The war had meant more than terrible death and destruction; it also brought a sense of change, of reluctant maturity to Canada and her people. During the war, all Canadians whether they were in French trenches or in Canadian factories, fields and homes had felt the strain of fierce extremes as love and hate, pride and sloth, fear and valour emerged full-blown as they never had before.

For such immoderate years, the dour and constant Robert Borden seemed an inappropriate leader. Ponderous in speech and plodding in movement, Borden knew that his chief virtues were his patience and honesty, scarcely the distinctions of the period. He was a Nova Scotian whose political career began as the stature of the Maritimes in the Canadian Confederation was steadily diminishing. Elected for the Halifax constituency in 1896, Borden's formative political years coincided with Canada's greatest national adventure, the opening of the Canadian West. After he became leader of the Conservative opposition in 1901, Borden, a farm boy, tried to persuade his Ontario-centred party to come to terms with the problems of rapid urbanization and industrialization. He was not fully successful, and when he was elected Prime Minister of Canada in 1911, he found his party and the Canadian parliamentary system to be a torpid behemoth that would rarely budge. But the war

7

transformed all this, and made remarkable political and economic change both possible and necessary. Soon, the war-time current of change threatened to become a flood that would sweep away much that was good. Borden's task then was to regulate this turbulence, to assure that war brought amelioration and not merely national and personal tragedy.

The responsibility was great, and Borden himself sometimes doubted his suitability for his position. He did not possess the vigour and zeal of youth; he turned sixty years of age in the first year of the war. Nor did he have that power which Pericles, Napoleon and Churchill summoned to spur their peoples towards new heights. Yet, among the allied leaders of August 1914, Borden alone endured the war, remaining at the centre of the Canadian political stage until 1920. To what can we attribute this exceptional endurance, and is endurance any criterion for success? In a larger sense, was Borden a catalyst or a soporific for those forces of change that transformed Canada in the second decade of the twentieth century? These are the central questions in this study of Robert Borden and his times.

In framing these questions, the work of Professor R. C. Brown on Robert Borden has been an invaluable guide. Professor Brown has generously allowed me to consult many references which I would not otherwise have seen. Dr. W. Kaye Lamb's great knowledge of Canadian history has made him an exemplary editor for this series, and this manuscript has benefited greatly from his perceptive comments. Robin Brass and Jim Shepherd of McGraw-Hill Ryerson have also provided useful advice. My wife has been both helpful and patient during the writing of this book and to her it is dedicated.

J.R.E.
Waterloo, Ont., 1977

OPPOSITE
Robert Borden in 1901, the year he became Leader of the Conservative Party.
Public Archives Canada,
PA-25942.

8

1
Canada in 1911

Before automobiles became common, excursion steamers offered one of the most popular means of taking an outing. Here the sidewheeler *Chippewa* is shown at Wards Island, in Toronto Harbour. *Metropolitan Toronto Library Board.*

"CANADA IS THE BRIGHTEST GEM IN THE CROWN OF THE BRITISH EMPIRE." By 1911, Sir Wilfrid Laurier's 1902 boast seemed less hyberbole than shrewd prophecy, for never had the Canadian jewel in the Imperial diadem gleamed so brilliantly. Individually and collectively, Canadians radiated the confidence born in the first tide of material prosperity. The first thirty years of Confederation had been difficult: the nation had grown but not quickly; some of her citizens had prospered but not many. Too often the young men left Ontario, Quebec or the Maritimes, drawn by the irresistible siren of industrial America and its high wages. Now they were staying in Canada and seeking adventure and affluence from the

Max Aitken, one of the millionaires produced by the boom years in Canada. He moved to England, where he was made a baronet in 1916 and was raised to the peerage as Baron Beaverbrook in 1917.
Public Archives Canada, C-47345.

opening of the Canadian West. As the young Canadians travelled westward, they regaled the many British immigrants beside them on the train with tales of fortunes made, lost and recovered. More often than is usual, these stories were true.

The young men from New Brunswick probably spun the best yarns about R. B. Bennett and Max Aitken, two of their fellow provincials who made their mark and fortune in the West. Bennett had left his first profession, teaching, to pursue a career at the bar. At the age of twenty-seven, the solemn, teetotaling Bennett decided to try his luck in freewheeling Calgary. The meeting of opposites was successful. Within a year, Bennett sat in the Legislative Assembly of the Northwest

R. B. Bennett, one of the easterners who made his fortune in the burgeoning West. After his move to Calgary, and before his thirty-fifth birthday, Bennett had become a millionaire.
*Public Archives Canada,
C-3869.*

Lawren Harris's landscapes, Arctic scenes
and abstracts have made such an impression
that many are unaware that in an earlier period
he was fascinated by cities, and in particular
by older and somewhat grubby districts of
Toronto.
The Gas Works was painted in 1911 or 1912.
Art Gallery of Ontario.

Emily Carr's painting, *Memalilaqua, Knight Inlet*,
depicts an Indian village in British Columbia. She was
fascinated by Indian houses and totem poles, and their
settings beside the forests and the sea. When this picture
was painted, in 1912, she had gained no recognition and
was working in what amounted to artistic isolation
in Victoria.
The National Gallery of Canada, Ottawa.

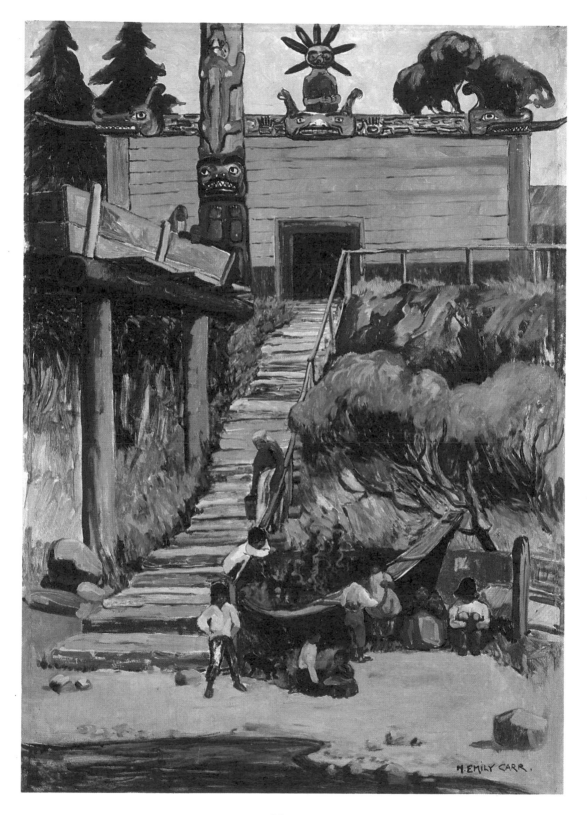

The new prairie provinces of Saskatchewan and Alberta lost little time in erecting imposing buildings to house their governments. This legislative building in Regina was completed in 1911.
Archives of Saskatchewan.

Territories and had become a leader of the Calgary bar. And fortune soon followed prestige and political success; before his thirty-fifth birthday, Bennett was a millionaire as well as a figure to reckon with on the national scene.

The path of Bennett's young, irreverent friend, Max Aitken, was even more remarkable. In 1902 the twenty-two-year-old Aitken set out to make himself a millionaire with only puckish charm and verve as his assets. Four years later, "Max" had his million dollars, and, like a good imperialist, he was determined to have his million pounds. They came much more quickly and so did acclaim and power. By 1910 Canada could not contain this young business wizard, and he left to conquer new worlds in Great Britain. At the end of his first year in Britain, thirty-year-old Max Aitken sat in the Mother of Parliaments, and the brilliant public career of Lord Beaverbrook had auspiciously begun.

For most Canadians, the careers of men like "Max" and "R. B." were ideals that brightened the glow of the imperial gem. But not all agreed. Some Canadians and quite a few foreign visitors pointed out that however brilliant the facade, the "Canadian gem" lacked internal consistency. Some might have their success, but what gains accrued to society as a whole from the individual gain? Nor could it be denied that for many, there was only failure and deprivation. Archibald Lampman provided the texts for the dissenters with two poems, "To a Millionaire" and "The Modern Politician." "But I," Lampman chastised the millionaire,

> Think only of the unnumbered broken hearts,
> The hunger and the mortal strife for bread,
> Old age and youth alike mistaught, misfed
> By want and rags and homelessness made vile,
> The griefs and hates, and all the meaner parts
> That balance thy one grim misgotten pile.

Even worse, the politician, the guardian of the public weal, was merely the puppet of the millionaire, serving his interest, protecting the grim misgotten pile. What sad specimens these politicians were!

> To them faith, kinship, truth and verity,
> Man's sacred rights and very holiest thing,
> Are but the counters at a desperate play,
> Flippant and reckless what the end may be,
> So that they glitter, each his little day,
> The little mimic of a vanished king.

Workers carving capitals for pillars in the legislative building in Edmonton, completed in 1911. It rivalled the Saskatchewan building in size and splendor. *Glenbow-Alberta Institute, Calgary, Alberta.*

Lampman despised his Trinity College classmates, now prominent businessmen or professionals, who had little time, except for a few moments on a Sunday morning, for the spiritual side of man. Canada, the critics charged, worshipped not the muses, only the demon Mammon.

Canadians may not have worshipped the muses because they scarcely knew them. Canadian universities were not the proud guardians of the nation's cultural heritage but mainly training institutions for professionals. Canada's honoured artists were at best derivative, at worst, comical; and, in fact, few Canadian artists were honoured at all by their countrymen. As one Canadian art collector told the young A. Y. Jackson, "It's bad enough to have to live in this country without having pictures of it in your home." For most Canadian collectors, Jackson recalled, art meant a cow or a windmill, painted by a Dutchman, surrounded by heavy gold frames and covered with plate glass with a spotlight over it. This meant social prestige and, one hoped, a solid investment. But if Jackson's 1910 painting, "The Edge of the Maple Wood" was unknown to or loathed by most Canadians, so too was Picasso's 1907 "Demoiselles d'Avignon" and, for that matter, the work of most of the significant painters of the age. Art and literature were afterthoughts, even for educated Canadians, and scholarship was the vocation of a very few. With the important exception of religion, there was little debate about ideas and what there was was conducted in rarefied isolation. Pre-war Canadians remained largely mute as Americans heatedly debated pragmatism, and they had learned nothing from Freud about the interpretation of their dreams, a decade after the publication of the Austrian's seminal study. The current of modernism which was sweeping Europe left barely a trickle in Canada. Canada, the pre-war tourist Rupert Brooke observed, seemed a country without a soul.

Had either Max Aitken or R. B. Bennett read Lampman's poetry or heard Brooke's comments, they would have thought them silly and would have added that few Canadians listened to such twaddle. They would have said that Brooke and Lampman had misunderstood the nature of business, of businessmen and of national greatness. The businessman was not solely or even mainly concerned with the accumulation of wealth; his purposes were patriotic and ultimately humanitarian. The success of the great business leaders set examples in hard work, character and public service for young Canadians, no matter how poor. No wonder a journalist could write that

"in the knapsack of every Canadian schoolboy there is — not a marshal's baton — but a millionaire's bankbook." The schoolboy knew better than Lampman and Brooke: what was good for capital was good for labour, the arts, and the nation. It was all so simple. Canada might have her poor and might lack a distinguished literature, but development and prosperity were building a foundation for future riches in all things. After all, Beaverbrook, a son of the manse, would say, a soul cannot survive without a healthy body, at least in its earthly state.

Most Canadians whatever their origin or social class agreed with Bennett and Aitken. Public confidence and optimism reigned supreme even in those locales where affluence had not yet found its place, for even the poor and the newcomer believed that their children and their grandchildren would live in abundance and peace. The Ukrainian or Austrian who had fled the Czar's or the Emperor's army thought that his children were forever isolated from the terrible turmoil and uncertainty of the old world. For this, a father would learn a new language, work long hours in the field or the factory, and leave old friends and family. The newcomer might struggle against prejudice, deprivation and greed, but there remained an exuberance and a sense of participation in a great adven-

Horse-drawn wagons, carriages and sleighs were still common when Borden become Prime Minister in 1911, but automobiles and trucks were replacing them rapidly by the time he resigned in 1920. *Notman Photographic Archives, McCord Museum of McGill University.*

A typical classroom in an elementary school about 1912 — plain and unadorned. Double desks were then being frowned upon and would soon give way to individual desks. *Public Archives of Nova Scotia.*

ture. Few others would ever have the opportunity to experience a young nation's discovery of her vitality, power and identity. If history meant anything, and both scholars and the public at the time believed it did, Canada was entering a new golden age, just as England had four centuries before. The shape of the future was uncertain but its bountifulness was not in doubt. "With glowing hearts we see thee rise,/The true north strong and free." R. Stanley Weir's 1909 poem, later Canada's national anthem, caught the spirit of the age.

This optimism flowed from many streams including some of foreign origin. First, there was a new configuration to world politics and Canada occupied a more secure place in it. Secondly, Imperialism, Social Darwinism, and early twentieth century geopolitics all pointed to Canada as a nation with a charmed future. Thirdly, economic and population growth in Canada during the first ten years of the twentieth century was more impressive than that of any other nation in the world. By examining the sources of Canadian optimism, we can comprehend how Canadians thought, lived, and worked in 1911.

Canadian Confederation had been, in large part, the product of American intimidation of British North America. From the early Loyalists through the Fathers of Confederation and beyond, Canadians had feared invasion from the south, often with good reason. Many Canadians still alive in 1900 could recall the defence of their native soil against the Fenian brotherhood; most recalled the threats of annexation emanating from within and without the nation in the 1880s and the 1890s. Great Britain had traditionally protected Canada against American malevolence but, paradoxically, the price of British protection had been the lasting threat of war. As every nineteenth century Canadian knew, Britain was her former American colony's traditional enemy and any Anglo-American disagreement could become a Canadian-American war. This had happened in 1812 and had almost happened again in the 1840s and the 1860s. The military threat was less after Confederation, but the political bluster of border state congressmen as well as the disillusionment of many Canadians with the progress of their own country frightened those who devoutly believed in a separate Canadian state.

In the late 1890s and the early 1900s, however, the situation subtly changed. Britain and the United States began to see more clearly their common interests and to value more highly their common heritage. At least part of this new perception arose from Victorian popular and academic theories about race and national character, a subject to which we will return later. What is important here is the two-fold Canadian reaction to Anglo-American rapprochement. On the one hand, Canada gained a new sense of security as war between Britain and the United States became a remote possibility. On the other hand, Canada realized that it could no longer depend upon Britain for defence or diplomatic support against the United States. Britain would sacrifice her Dominion's interest if it were necessary to maintain her invaluable friendship with the United States. This truth was bluntly demonstrated by the Alaska Boundary Tribunal's decision in 1903. This tribunal had been set up to adjudicate a long-standing boundary dispute on the Pacific Coast, and was made up of three Americans, two Canadians and one British member, Lord Alverstone. The final vote, four to two in favour of the American case, showed that nationality and fear had triumphed over judicial impartiality. What infuriated the Canadians was not the decision itself but Lord Alverstone's open capitulation to American pressure. The lesson for the future was clear and Laurier stated

Street urchins in Winnipeg in 1912. Bare feet were often due to lack of shoes rather than choice.
Public Archives Canada, C-30951.

it in the House of Commons: "We have at last come to the conclusion that . . . we would do better by attending to the business ourselves rather than having it trusted to the best men that can be found in Great Britain."

Canadians soon found that they could do very well indeed

Youngsters of nine or over were employed in this British Columbia mine as mule boys.
B. J. Knight. Public Archives Canada, C-56705.

by attending to their own business. Most of the outstanding differences in Canadian-American relations were cleared up by 1912. The institutional symbol of the new era of cooperation between Canada and the United States was the Interna-

The Superintendent of Neglected Children in Manitoba included this picture of a 14-year-old coal miner in his annual report for 1912.
Public Archives Canada, C-30945.

tional Joint Commission, a still-existing body that seeks to settle boundary disputes by peaceful means. What might have become a cause for despair, the withdrawal of British tutelage and protection, had instead become a source of new self-confidence. Never had Canadian-American relations been so good, and Canadians themselves had been instrumental in achieving this end. In 1911, this new amity led to a reciprocity trade agreement between Canada and the United States. Although the anti-reciprocity Conservatives won that election, after a campaign which featured unfortunate statements on both sides of the forty-ninth parallel, Canadian-American friendship remained intact and Canadian ties with the United States continued to grow. A dramatic upheaval had destroyed the nineteenth century diplomatic landscape and had replaced it with a more congenial one for Canada.

As international political shifts favoured Canada, so too did turn of the century intellectual movements, the most influential of which was Imperialism. Imperialism is a term whose overuse in the latter part of the twentieth century has largely deprived it of meaning. In Canada in 1911, however, the meaning of Imperialism was well-known and quite specific: very simply, the Canadian Imperialists were those who favoured closer union among the component parts of the British Empire. This movement had sprung up in Canada to counter nineteenth century annexationist sentiment, but its heyday came when the threat of annexation had subsided and Canadian self-confidence prevailed. For, as Professor Carl Berger has shown in *The Sense of Power*, Canadian Imperialism was above all else a form of Canadian nationalism that rested upon a "sense of power," an interpretation of history that foresaw great things ahead for the Canadian nation. Imperialists believed that in any closer imperial union, Canada would play an increasingly important and, in time perhaps, the dominant part. The Imperialist press of Canada invariably depicted Britain as the weary Titan, exhausted by her world-wide responsibilities, and Canada as the fresh, strapping youth rushing to offer support. The humourist Stephen Leacock, himself a devout Imperialist, expressed this feeling well: "The old man's got old and he don't know it, can't kick him off the place, but I reckon that the next time we come together to talk things over, the boys have got to step right in and manage the farm." Here was the prospect that thrilled Canadian Imperialists: managing the "farm," the vast British Empire. What a responsibility! What an opportunity!

24

By the end of the century, Canadian Imperialists had achieved significant influence within English Canada. In 1899, Imperialist pressure compelled Sir Wilfrid Laurier to send a volunteer force to fight the Boers in South Africa and to defend the ideals and the interests of the Empire in that distant place. While the South African War received considerable criticism in Quebec, in non-British nations including the United States, and even in Britain itself, scarcely a note of dissent could be heard in English Canada where Imperialism had captured the imagination of the press and much of the public. As Canada's population swelled and her industries and

A Packard car in Montreal in the winter of 1912. The proud owner is at the wheel and the chauffeur stands by, ready to crank the engine. Electric lights and starters were just being introduced. This car had acetylene headlights and oil side and tail lights. *Notman Photographic Archives, McCord Museum of McGill University.*

wealth burgeoned, the thought of an imperial and international mission for Canada fired the enthusiasm of the prosperous urban middle class. Here, it seemed, was a future for the nation consistent with its British past and redolent of greatness for the years to come. Opposition to Imperialism by French Canadians and by others was attacked as narrow minded parochialism. Imperialists disdainfully asked their critics if they really wanted Canada to bear forever the intellectual, moral, and physical limitations of her present state. Surely they didn't, no patriotic Canadian could. Leacock stated the essence of the Canadian Imperialist position in 1907: "I am an Imperialist, because I will not be a Colonial." Canada's colonial past was behind her; before her lay responsibility, eminence, and grandeur.

The justification of European Imperialism was closely linked with Social Darwinism and nineteenth century race thinking. The former ascribed the same evolutionary process which Darwin had found in biology to the evolution of human society. At its crudest, Social Darwinism asserted that the fittest would and should survive and that the weak must perish. In its more specific application, this meant that Britain and Canada had to fight to maintain the paramountcy of British

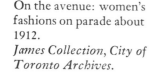

On the avenue: women's fashions on parade about 1912.
James Collection, City of Toronto Archives.

power. For might was right, and the power of the Empire was itself the best proof of the higher state of civilization of Britain and her Empire. If the Imperial peoples remained true to their ideals, there could be no doubt of future victories.

"Race thinking" was more complicated and laced with deeper shades of ambiguity. It was, nonetheless, a fundamental ingredient in Canadian Imperialism and in Canadian political and social decisions before World War I. This is not surprising, for in the nineteenth century race seemed the key to the understanding of historical development. Walter Bagehot, an influential English critic, had written in 1869 that "when a philosopher cannot account for anything in any other manner, he boldly ascribes it to an occult quality in some race." This was as true for the general public as for the philosopher. The "purity" and the "fitness" of the race were discussed everywhere; and once again Canadians saw their nation as especially favoured by fate. Negroes, the "lower" race so common in the United States, were rarely found in Canada. Southern Europeans, a "lazy," "impure" breed, were also few in number. In the main, Canada had peopled her fields and cities with a sturdy stock; the French peasant, the English

The Victorian notion of the gentility of ladies doing needlework is certainly reflected in this 1912 photo. Six years later, during the latter part of Borden's administration, complete enfranchisement of Canadian women in federal elections was accomplished.
Public Archives Canada, C-45390.

Immigrants waiting to come ashore at Quebec from the liner *Empress of Britain*. The picture was taken about 1912.
Public Archives Canada, PA-10235.

yeoman, and the Scottish crofter. English Canadians frequently pointed to the achievements of their race in government and in war as proof of their own higher stage of racial development. Race thinking, then, served to justify utopian visions of Canada's future and also, unfortunately, individual and national arrogance and prejudice.

Underlying these vague and unscientific notions of racial superiority and spiritual destiny was solid evidence of Canada's growth. To an age in which most people identified progress with growth, this evidence was most compelling. Much of the Canadian malaise before 1896 can probably be attributed to the slowness of population increase. Population growth was regarded as perhaps the most important determinant of national power and vitality. Macdonald's national policy, for example, had population increase as a key plank, but this promise was not immediately fulfilled. After the closing of the American frontier in 1896, an excellent immigration service and a booming economy with abundant jobs caused Canada's population to leap suddenly upwards. The 1901 census counted 5,371,315 Canadians and the 1911 census, 7,206,643. This was an increase of over 34 per cent, the highest of any decade in post-Confederation Canadian history. Even more striking was the growth of individual provinces and cities. In 1901, the area of Saskatchewan (it was not yet a province) had only 91,279 residents scattered singly or in small groups over the vast prairie. Ten years later, there were 492,432 people in Saskatchewan, already a province with independent authority, a thriving economy, a university, and a lively provincial capital with a political and social life of its own. In 1901, the capital, Regina, had been a village whose population was just over 2,000 and whose residents knew each other well — often too well. By 1911, Regina had become a city of 30,000, and on the main street, the 1901 resident would find that most passersby were strangers. In Saskatoon a downtown corner lot sold for $450 dollars in 1904 and $47,500 in 1911, and there were 150 real estate agents in a city of 10,000. Nor was it much different in Calgary and Edmonton in the new province of Alberta. Between 1901 and 1911, Calgary saw its population multiplied by 10 to 43,000. In Edmonton, however, growth was slower; the increase was only 750 per cent!

Ontario and Quebec also registered dramatic population increases in this period. Montreal became a city of international rank as its population soared from 267,730 in 1901 to 470,480 in 1911. Toronto, which had seemed on the verge of overtaking Montreal in the 1890's, fell farther behind her sister city between 1901 and 1911, although Toronto's population itself increased by over 80 per cent. Even the Maritimes, which

The great influx of immigrants in the years before the First World War was due in part to energetic promotion campaigns by the Government of Canada and the C.P.R. Government efforts in Great Britain were directed from these Emigration Offices in London.
Public Archives Canada, C-63257.

showed little overall growth, saw much change as the young men from farms and small towns left their homes for Halifax or Saint John, Toronto or Calgary.

What brought these Canadians to the cities? Obviously, there were a score of individual reasons. In the case of the Eastern cities, the magnet was primarily the factories and the financial institutions. On the prairies, agriculture remained the economic mainstay, and a town like Regina was either a parasite on, or the controlling brain of, the Saskatchewan wheat economy, depending on one's viewpoint. In British Columbia, Vancouver became a major port and a metropolitan centre for an immensely rich hinterland. Whatever the activity, wherever it took place, the first ten years of the new century were almost invariably better than any previous decade. Prices were excellent, and productivity and profits rose constantly. The gross national product, that well-known measure of a nation's economic health, more than doubled between 1900 and 1910. Those with the skills that maintained the economy's momentum reaped great reward. The Montreal plumber's average wage rose from eighteen to thirty-five cents per hour. The labourer did not do so well; his average wage rose only from fifteen to twenty-two cents per hour. This itself is an indication of the increasing sophistication of the Canadian economy and of the value of special training. Still,

Eighth Avenue, Calgary, in 1912.
Glenbow-Alberta Institute, Calgary, Alberta.

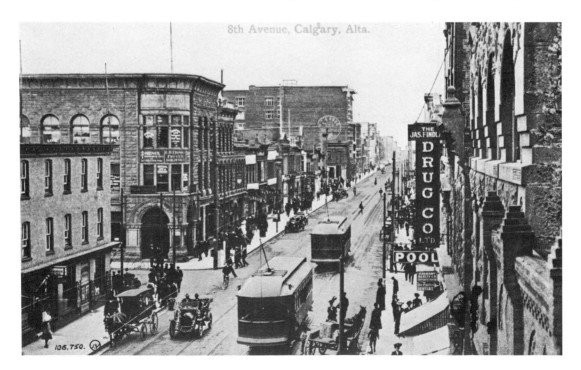

there were abundant opportunities for the labourer in the "New West" where he could try his hand at wheat farming; the price for a bushel had never been so high. And if farming were not to his taste, the labourer might go to "New Ontario" whose mineral riches were just beginning to be tapped. The possibilities for Canada and Canadians seemed limitless.

The fecundity of native Canadians could not satisfy the incessant demand for men to work in the fields and factories of Canada. The government, the factory owner, the miner, and even the individual farmer had to look abroad for new sources of labour. Under the direction of Clifford Sifton, Laurier's ablest minister, Canadian immigration agents scoured Northern Europe and Russia for hardy young men and their families. Their success was sudden and remarkable: whole communities packed up and came to Canada, mostly to the West. In 1901, 55,000 immigrants arrived, the largest number in 10 years. Four years later in 1905, there were almost three times as many, and in 1911 over six times as many, as 333,225 newcomers made Canada their home. The extraordinary scale of immigration between 1901 and 1911 is best illustrated by the 10-year total of approximately 1,750,000 immigrants, a num-

Jasper Avenue East, Edmonton, in 1914. *Glenbow-Alberta Institute, Calgary, Alberta.*

ber equal to almost 40 per cent of Canada's 1901 population. Yet, as immigrant ships discharged their human cargo at Quebec and Halifax, many Canadians — over a million between 1901 and 1911 — crossed the border to begin new lives in the United States. Everywhere there were men and women in motion.

What effect did this human tide have upon the Canada prairie? Ralph Connor's popular and sympathetic novel, *The Foreigner* (1909) captures the variety and the determination of the immigrant and portrays the profound impact of immigration on the Prairies, where so many "foreigners" joined Canadians making new homes. It also candidly outlines the new Canadian's future as it was envisaged by the native-born. While the immigrants themselves chose to live "segregated into colonies tight knit by ties of blood and common tongue," their children could not. "Out of breeds diverse in traditions, in ideals, in speech, and in manner of life" must come "one people." There could be no Canadian mosaic where separate growths could flourish and develop individual excellence. Instead, there would be a melting pot which would fuse together the varied peoples into one race, united in culture and attitude.

The land that promised so much to the immigrant demanded much as well. But it would be wrong to think that the immigrant's difficulties in adjusting to an alien environment were unique. Was the experience of the French Canadian who came from a rural parish to a Montreal factory that was owned and managed by English Canadians, less painful than that of the Ukrainian, Scandinavian, or Scot who broke the prairie sod? All evidence suggests it was not. Nor did the southwestern Ontario farmboy who went to work in the local factory find it easy to accept the regularity, the stratification and the monotony of industrial life. And as work conditions changed so did social conditions. Urban workers born in farmhouses might have to live in urban tenements where their neighbours were only nameless faces and where there was little hope of improvement. The expansion of the cities had created an acute housing crisis, appalling sanitary conditions, and embarrassing municipal corruption that made reform nearly impossible.

Throughout Canada but especially in the New West, the human tide created its own waves which temporarily overwhelmed the fragile structures of religion, law and tradition. The West was a hard society, a male society of a coarse grain

OPPOSITE
Borden portraits abound. In this stately photograph of 1901, Borden is seated at the desk which served as a prop in the Topley Studio photographs of several famous Canadian men including Sir John A. Macdonald and D'Arcy McGee.
Public Archives Canada, PA-12273.

First and second houses on the prairies. The original house, on the right, built of squared timbers and with a thatch roof, has been succeeded by a frame dwelling with a shingle roof.
Manitoba Archives.

where the bar and the brothel flourished. "By the summer of 1910," James Gray writes, "the Winnipeg red-light district had degenerated into a massive orgiastic obscenity. The sky-rocketing Winnipeg population, coupled with the tremendous floating population kept the district on a twenty-four-hour-shift all through the summer."* Sometimes there were raids; in 1912 in Calgary the police raided many of the "gilded palaces of hollow laughter" in which, a reporter declaimed,

> Rouge paint and powder could not conceal the unmistake-able traces of dissipation. That sin had collected at least part of its wages was apparent to even the most casual observer. The sunken eyes, some of them brilliant from belladonna, and hollow cheeks told a story of riotous living that could not be denied.

Soon the gilded palaces opened again, for Calgary had no jail to hold the prostitutes. In a sense, the police reporter was cor-

*James H. Gray, *Red Lights on the Prairies* (Toronto, Macmillan, 1971), p. 50. Gray also points out that Police Chief Marwick of Medicine Hat owned the house in which the town's main brothel ran for four years.

rect; the laughter was hollow. The brothels were overcrowded, vulgar, and nearly always unsanitary, while the girls were often immigrants thrown by poverty and unfamiliarity into the trade or even children abandoned by fate or family. Golden hearts there may have been, but the life of a prostitute was mostly sordid and invariably sad.

Prostitution, of course, preceded the period of rapid growth; so did poverty. Even before the unprecedented post-1900 population boom, a survey of a working class area of Montreal carried out in 1897 by Herbert Ames had revealed overcrowding, poverty and sanitary facilities worse than anyone had imagined. The aristocratic, Harvard educated Ames was shocked to learn "that that relic of rural conditions, that insanitary abomination, the out-of-door-pit-in-the-ground privy, is still to be found in the densely populated heart of the city." Indeed, more than half of the households within the area surveyed depended upon that "privy pot abomination." Ames found one area that had over three hundred residents per acre living in squalor which would inevitably breed disease and discontent. In the worst district, Griffintown, one out of four families earned less than the five dollars a week which Ames estimated to be necessary for mere subsistence. These people were not drones, feckless souls who shunned all responsibility; they wanted permanent jobs but could not find them. Not imbecility, not lethargy, but irregularity of work was the major cause of poverty: "Once irregular always irregular, . . . and irregularity, demoralization and poverty is the order of descent."

The conditions of crowding might have been much worse had not the expansion of trolley lines, and later, the development of the automobile and the motor bus permitted many urban dwellers to live far from their place of work. The urban reformer and Methodist clergyman, J. S. Woodsworth, regarded the new transportation improvements as the key to the alleviation of urban woes. "Multiply transportation facilities," Woodsworth wrote, "and every citizen may own his own suburban home — yes, and do his work in a district that resembles a park rather than a jungle." Woodsworth proved to be a poor prophet. The freedom that the automobile gave was largely limited to the middle class, and the suburbs became the refuge from the cares of the office and the problems of the city for middle class Canadians. The poor simply could not afford to move to the single family dwellings that made up suburban communities. The face of Canadian cities was thereby fundamentally altered, and poverty and prosperity became more clearly defined.*

Ames' study, *The City Below the Hill*, was written for those citizens in the city above the hill, Montrealers of means who often knew far more about foreign lands than about the poor areas of their own city. The city above the hill with its pleasant walks, its grand homes, its domestic servants and private bathrooms gained greatly in area, population and splendour as Montreal's commercial, financial and industrial life advanced. Not only in Montreal but in every Canadian community, this thriving middle class was the most visible and articulate element, and it was this class that endowed Canada with its optimistic hue. Their journalistic spokesmen such as the *Busy Man's Magazine*, the *Canadian Magazine* and the *Manitoba Free Press* reflected their confidence, prosperity and curiosity in both articles and advertising. For example, the January 1911 issue of the *Canadian Magazine* contained a paean to the Toronto Board of Trade Building, an article on the "smart set" of Ottawa, and another on the plays of the Broadway and the London season. The pretension and boosterism of the articles was also present in the advertisements. Buy a gramophone, "the ideal entertainment for the long winter evenings"; or, even better, take the "Santa Fe all the way" to "Senorita California where January is like June." If you stayed north, all was not lost: for nineteen hundred dollars you could own a five-passenger McLaughlin-Buick whose thirty-five horsepower would whisk you home from skating or parties on a cold winter's night.

But all these things, the automobile, the gramophone, the southern tour, and maybe even the *Canadian Magazine* itself were beyond the reach of many Canadians. The Griffintown worker's five dollars a week would not permit much more than basic subsistence, yet the popular press, the new moving pictures, and the billboards all stressed the desirability and ubiquity of consumption and luxury. For the moment, general prosperity inspired the dream that, through mass produc-

*Recent research has confirmed that the urban poor derived little benefit from early twentieth century Canadian growth. See Terry Copp, *The Anatomy of Poverty: The Condition of the Working Class in Montreal 1897-1929* (Toronto, McClelland and Stewart, 1974), and Michael Piva, "The Condition of the Working Class in Toronto, 1900-1921" (Ph.D. thesis, Concordia University, 1975).

On July 25, 1911, Bobby Leach conquered Niagara Falls in this barrel which clearly shows the effects of his perilous trip.
Public Archives Canada, C-14062.

tion and education, the future would bring richness for all. This belief acted as a soporific that benumbed class antagonism, but thoughtful Canadians realized that this effect would not endure forever. Poverty, disease and prejudice were enemies of order and freedom that could not be allowed to gain. In 1911, Canada acquired a new commander in its battle against these ancient foes. For the next decade, the fate of the Empire's brightest gem lay in the hands of a middle-aged Nova Scotian lawyer, Robert Laird Borden.

2
Robert Borden, 1854-1911

In 1854, Ottawa, soon to be the new capital of Canada's united provinces, was no more than a bustling frontier lumber town, and the Canadian Confederation was merely a glint in the eyes of a few visionaries. Yet Grand Pré, where Eunice Laird Borden gave birth to a son, Robert Laird, was renowned throughout the literary world, from the drawing rooms of London to the coffee houses of Boston. The poet Longfellow's "Evangeline," a timeless tale of the heroic and constant love of two young Acadians, had caught the fancy of a romantic age. In Longfellow's poem, Grand Pré where "Gentle Evangeline" lived was a village of haunting beauty and personal harmony. Although "naught but tradition" remained of the Acadian settlement by 1854, the new village still possessed the same arresting charm. Many years later, Robert Borden recalled the land where he was born and raised:

> Across the interval of seventy years, there is still fresh and vivid in my memory the outlook, the orchards, the upland fields, the distant meadows, and the quiet village streets with their fine Lombardy poplars and old willows. I can hear the surf on the shores of Long Island, which lay north of the Grand Pré meadow and the soughing of the south wind in the evening often lulling me to sleep.

Neither time nor man has yet destroyed the loveliness of Evangeline's "hallowed ground."

Robert Borden was of the conqueror's race: the first Bordens had arrived in King's County, Nova Scotia, before the American Revolution and long before the great influx of the Loyalists. Apparently the Bordens were quite numerous by the 1850s, but they were not very notable. Arthur Meighen,

OPPOSITE
Robert Borden, aged five.

39

Borden's parents: Andrew Borden, and his remarkable mother, Eunice Laird Borden.

a friend and colleague of Robert, pointed out that no adventitious fortune lay in young Robert's path and like most young Nova Scotians of the day, he had to make his own way in an often harsh world. Borden's father, Andrew, had settled down to become the station master at Grand Pré after an unsuccessful attempt at a business career. By his own and by his son's standards, Andrew Borden was not a successful man. In his memoirs, Robert Borden's portrait of his father is vaguely drawn, but that of his mother has the imprint of life. She was, Borden recalled, a woman of very strong character, remarkable energy, high ambition, and unusual ability; one who was con-

spicuous in any company. Doubtless, the strength of Eunice Borden's character in her son's eyes was enhanced by the weakness of her husband.

Modern psychology might see this background as pregnant in meaning for our understanding of the character of Robert Borden, but unfortunately our knowledge is insufficient for such an analysis. It would be wrong to make too much of Borden's image of his parents. It should also be noted that while Robert possessed strong self-discipline, intensity and seriousness, his brother, Henry, was fun-loving, irresponsible and flighty. Whatever the sources of Borden's per-

Henry Clifford Borden, one of Sir Robert's brothers.

sonality, its traits were well-defined at an early age. At twelve, we are told, Borden began reflecting upon the meaning of existence. So dedicated was young "Rob" to his studies that he drew up timetables to chart his day, a passion which even his mother ridiculed. This prodigious intellectual energy, however, was not channelled through formal educational systems. Borden's knowledge forever retained the eclectic pattern of the self-educated, which was by no means a disadvantage for a public man of his time. Still, there was a price: in cultural terms, Borden was limited, never acquiring an informed acquaintance with the art and literature of both past and present. He would attend concerts and plays, but afterwards in his diary, he would merely list the title, never offer a comment. He taught himself Latin and mastered the conjugations of the most difficult verbs, but it was the mechanics and not the literary expression of the language which fascinated Borden. In this, he undoubtedly reflected the spirit of most of his Canadian contemporaries. It was, nevertheless, a source of enduring regret.

After attending a boarding school for several years where standards were sufficiently low that he became an assistant master at the age of fourteen, Borden, like so many of his contemporaries, decided that greater opportunity lay to the south. In 1873, he became assistant master at Glenwood Institute in Matawan, New Jersey. He remained in New Jersey only one year, and, although he claimed to have enjoyed his stay, he never returned, not even for a day. If New Jersey could not offer the young teacher what he wanted neither could his former home in Grand Pré. He therefore chose to settle in Nova Scotia's cosmopolitan capital, Halifax.

The early 1870s had not been kind to Halifax as steam replaced wind as the major propellant of world transportation. Halifax had thrived during the age of sail, and her ships had roamed to the far corners of the British Imperial world as well as to the familiar, closer Yankee ports of Boston and New York. The 1873 death of Joseph Howe, Nova Scotia's most eloquent voice, had symbolized the city's changing circumstances. Reciprocity, always the source of great profit in the

When Borden was four, the family moved to this home in Grand Pré.

Pinehurst in Halifax. The
success of Borden's law
practice was reflected in
the grandeur of this home.
During the early political
days letters between Laura
at Pinehurst and Robert
in Ottawa were warm and
frequent. In 1905, the
Bordens gave up Pinehurst
and took up residence in
Ottawa — a sign that
politics had become a
full-time profession.
H. A. Buckmaster.

past, now seemed far beyond the grasp of the young Canadian Confederation. Confederation — or botheration as Howe had called it — had forced Haligonians to look towards the West and to the Intercolonial Railway that would bind Halifax with the inland cities of central Canada. Perhaps the future would see Halifax as the great winter outlet for the ice-bound St. Lawrence ports, but the Haligonians were not especially confident that this would occur. "Upper Canada" had given them nothing in the past; why should they expect it now? If the Haligonians were disgruntled with their future prospects, they were nonetheless pleased with their city's past achievements and present state. The city had only thirty thousand residents, but her schools, her Academy of Music

The Bordens had no children, but young Henry Borden, son of Sir Robert's brother Henry, became almost like a son to them.

and her imposing homes were the match for those in any Canadian city. Moreover, Haligonians would point out, the British garrison had brought the sophistication of the motherland to their city and made Halifax's "proper society" superior to that of frontier Toronto and even old Montreal. And its "improper society" was proud as well, for the many girls of "Barrack Street" were the equal of any along the Atlantic's shore.

What could a serious and talented young man do in this city? Teaching had apparently lost its charm for Robert Borden and of the few other respectable callings only a legal career seemed attractive. He thought of Ontario but his mother urged Halifax, and Halifax it would be. When he arrived in the city in 1874, Dalhousie's law school had not yet been founded, and legal training was obtained through a system of apprenticeship under which students were articled to practising lawyers.

For Borden, such a form of education may have been of mediocre quality but at least it was possible. The formalization of professional training, of which he was later a strong supporter, tended to restrict entry to the professions to the sons of the prosperous and to keep out the sons of station masters. In 1874, however, Borden had no difficulty in finding an articling position. Living on the meagre wages that it bestowed, Borden soon found that his training valued industry above intelligence. Since he possessed both, the former in abundance, Borden did well. Of course there was doubt and discouragement. He wrote to his mother, his closest and perhaps his only confidant, on a stormy New Year's morn in 1877:*

> 1876 is no more. I can remember of looking forward to it, in 1870, and thinking "how old will I be if I live till then." I determined to accomplish much before the time came round for I did not wish to be two and twenty and an ignoramus. Well the time has come and gone, and how little has been accomplished. The chariot wheels of time have rolled all too swiftly for my tardy efforts.

Ambition driven by doubt, achievement tempered by evanescence, these fears stayed with Borden, though in the

*Interestingly, no letters to or from Borden's father survive although the correspondence with his mother endures. It possesses a warmth and candour absent in later documents, including Borden's diary.

future they were seldom expressed. External recognition was
a most efficacious palliative, and in 1877 Borden won such
recognition when he stood first in the Nova Scotia bar ex-
aminations. He must have derived special pleasure when he
learned that Charles Hibbert Tupper, the son of Nova Scotia's
greatest politician, stood below him.

The young Tupper was certainly impressed by Borden
and he remembered him; five years after their graduation, he
invited Borden to join his prestigious firm, Graham and Tupper, as a junior partner. Suddenly, new legal, personal and
political worlds opened to Borden as he began presenting
cases before the Supreme Court of Canada in Ottawa and even

before the august Judicial Committee of the Privy Council in London. As his partners departed, Graham for the bench and Tupper for politics, Borden acquired pre-eminence in the firm and in Nova Scotian legal circles generally. There is no evidence that his prodigious appetite for work diminished, but, in 1889, he did permit himself a pleasure too long denied: he married Laura Bond, the daughter of a Halifax businessman. Elegance, affluence and decorum marked the style of these rather old newlyweds. Laura Borden was Robert's lifelong companion, but it is doubtful that home was ever his major interest. Laura and Robert were to have no family, and, far from forcing Borden to husband his resources and time,

Halifax in 1887: the city as Robert Borden knew it as a rising young lawyer who would soon have the most prosperous law practice in the Maritimes. *Public Archives Canada, PA-31176.*

marriage appears to have facilitated his deeper involvement in his legal, business and political careers.

This, of course, was typical of an age when the domestic ideal was the cornerstone of the middle class value system. Robert enjoyed Laura; she had a sense of fun and character. Certainly they loved each other. They chatted and even confided; but they did not discuss. Discussion came with men at the militia or the club, over Scotch, with close friends. Discussion possessed a hearty, earthy texture foreign to conversation with women. With a Charlie Tupper or a George Perley or other men, Borden was exuberant, swore and took delight in skewering opponents, but this was private. Men and women, public and private; the distinctions were clear and, to Borden, important. The home was a retreat, a refuge; the public performance, only a cautious and partial revelation. One ordered one's life, one accepted patterns, one feared failure most of all.

Material success mattered very much and this Borden achieved very early. By the early 1890s, Borden's law practice had become the largest in the Maritimes, and his income was as high as thirty thousand dollars per year at a time when a day labourer's yearly income was less than three hundred dollars. The rewards of success, the fine home, prestige and important local office, came quickly. Through hard work, intelligence and persistence, Robert Borden had conquered the once forbidding garrison of Halifax. Moreover, youth was still his ally and was prodding him towards larger goals. Inevitably, one of these was politics.

In nineteenth century Canada, the relationship between the political backroom and the courthouse was very close; too close most would say. Borden's two partners were involved in politics, one of them most actively. In the House of Commons, lawyers had outnumbered all other callings since the time of Confederation. Furthermore, in Nova Scotia, politics ran through the blood of the native born. Nevertheless, Borden claimed that he had little interest in politics until he was approached by Tupper. This may be true, but the more likely reason for Borden's reticence about his early political activities was his inherited Liberalism. Not only had his parents rallied to the Liberal banners, but his cousin, Frederick Borden, was a prominent Nova Scotian Liberal, and a federal cabinet minister after 1896. Not surprisingly, Borden's first political appearance was on a Liberal campaign platform with his cousin; the date, unfortunately, is unknown.

51

Glensmere, the imposing Ottawa residence purchased by Borden in 1906. It was to be his home for over thirty years. The house, built in 1894, was designed by the architect who planned the elaborate interior of the Library of Parliament. This photograph was taken about 1913.

According to his memoirs, Borden became a Conservative convert in 1886 when the Liberal Premier W. S. Fielding won the provincial election of that year on a platform of secession from Confederation. Although most historians regard Fielding's threat as a ploy to obtain better terms from the federal government, Borden almost certainly took Fielding's bluff seriously in 1886, by which time he had become a strong believer in Confederation.

To Borden, belief meant service. Thus when Canada's Prime Minister, Sir Charles Tupper, asked his son's friend, Robert Borden, to stand for election in 1896, Borden agreed to sacrifice his lucrative legal practice and try his hand in the political world. He nevertheless promised Tupper, Laura and himself that he would serve in Ottawa for only one term and then return to the Halifax that he loved. The pledge proved meaningless; politics were to be central in Borden's life for the next quarter century.

His distinguished political career began with a personal victory in the 1896 election as his party went down to embarrassing defeat. With his great thatch of graying hair parted precisely and elegantly in the middle, his sterling reputation at the bar preceding him, and his dignified bearing inspiring respect and confidence, the new member for Halifax stood out among freshmen Conservative Members in the new Parliament. Yet while he impressed, he failed to stir. Hearing

OPPOSITE
Mrs. Borden in 1901. After she moved to Ottawa much of the social life of the capital that was associated with politics centred around Lady Laurier and herself. *Public Archives Canada, PA-12277.*

Borden in the Commons reminded one man of wit of Goldsmith's couplet on Burke:

> Too deep for his hearers and always refining;
> He thought of convincing, while they thought of dining.

Lacking the eloquence of Laurier and Tupper, Borden had to depend upon thoroughness and his capacious memory to make his Parliamentary mark, although it is likely that his prestige with his colleagues also benefited from his old friendship with the Tuppers. What probably impressed Borden's fellow members most, however, were his extraordinary powers of concentration and his energy. During the four or five months of the parliamentary session Borden was "altogether a politician," and for the remainder of the year he was "altogether a practising lawyer," and he was eminently successful in both careers. By the end of his first Parliament, Borden had advanced to the Conservative front bench and had become a leader in the Conservative assault on the government of Sir Wilfrid Laurier.

While Robert boarded in Ottawa, Laura usually stayed at Pinehurst, their grand Halifax home. They wrote regularly and Laura's letters were always a most effective balm for his loneliness; but Robert's replies were sometimes little more than a sluice for his frustration. "This political life," he wrote in 1896, "seems to me most stale and flat and unprofitable. I am convinced that it is absolutely unsuited to a man of my temperament and the sooner I get out of it the better." To cheer him, Laura urged that he should come home "or I will have to come to you." But she didn't, and Robert's irritations festered: "It is a miserable irregular life that one has to lead and I am more than sick of it." His health suffered – a New York doctor put him on a special diet and warned him that he must slow down – but Borden could not let go. He told Laura that "unless I alter my mind greatly, nothing will induce me to again become a candidate." But when the election came,

Mrs. Borden in a formal portrait of 1909.
Public Archives Canada, PA-42519.

Robert Borden was once again a candidate and once again he won.

In the 1900 election, the "Cumberland war horse," Sir Charles Tupper, ran and lost his last political race. Who was to replace the Tories' seventy-nine-year-old leader? Tupper maintained sufficient vigour and guile to deny the succession to any of his numerous enemies, but not enough to secure it for his favourite, his son. Together, the Tuppers determined to pass on the mantle to an unquestioned loyalist, one untainted by involvement in the Conservative civil war which had followed Sir John A. Macdonald's death in 1891. Sir Charles Hibbert Tupper's nomination of his friend Robert Borden on February 5, 1901 undoubtedly shocked most of the seventy Conservative M.P.'s and Senators who had gathered to choose their new leader in a caucus room in the old centre block of the Parliament Buildings. A few of the Tory notables had scarcely heard of Borden, but they respected Tupper's right to name his successor so they voted for the relatively young and certainly politically inexperienced lawyer. By the end of the day, the Conservative caucus had given the new leader their unanimous support.

The choice was puzzling to politician and public alike. Why would the Conservatives pick a "dark horse," a political novice whose major qualification seemed to be his former legal partnership with Charles Hibbert Tupper? What impact would the quiet Nova Scotian, so unlike his boisterous predecessor and earlier Canadian Conservative leaders, have upon his party? Such questions lingered on not just for a few days, but for several years as Robert Borden made little apparent impression upon Canadian politics and the Conservative Party.

But the appearance was deceptive. In fact, Borden was a new type of political leader, the choice of the past but not a representative of it. Previously, Canadian politics had seemed like a circus with several performances going on simultaneously and the leader a flamboyant master of ceremonies. This was not Borden's style: he would not be found in the centre ring, but in the office counting the circus' receipts and giving overall rather than immediate direction. He could not accept that his role was simply to please the electorate, to play to its prejudices and fancies. How much better it would be, Borden thought, if political activity were primarily educational. Politics were too serious a business to be left to the politicians, including those on the Conservative benches behind him.

OPPOSITE
Arthur Meighen in 1912, when he was still a backbencher. He would become Solicitor-General the following year, would join Borden's cabinet in 1915, and would succeed him as Prime Minister only five years later.
Public Archives Canada,
PA-26987.

HELPING SAM.

Sir Wilfrid—"Whoa, now; Sam wants to milk you."

An anti-reciprocity cartoon published in the Vancouver *Province* shortly before the election of 1911.

But if Borden had doubts, he still proceeded with caution in changing the contours of the party which he had inherited. There were small changes; one of the first of these was consultations with Canadians outside Parliament who shared Borden's views on the proper role of the politician. Within the Commons chamber itself, he established a reputation as a virulent critic of political corruption. New men were encouraged to accept their moral responsibility and to elevate the tone of party politics. Unfortunately Borden's rhetoric had a hollow ring after an embarrassing incident which occurred during the 1904 election campaign, his first as party leader. Through that inveterate political conspirator, Hugh Graham, the publisher of the *Montreal Star*, Borden became involved in an extraordinary plot, which included bribery of journalists, resignations of Quebec Liberal candidates late in the campaign, and large contributions to the Conservative party in exchange for certain promises. The plan was as foolish as it was wrong. Naturally it failed and so did Borden. The Liberals won a decisive victory in the election of 1904.*

Both the defeat and the Graham scheme greatly disturbed Borden and they certainly should have. We now know that he had lied to the Canadian people during the campaign about his involvement in the Graham plot; perhaps even more troubling, he had also lied to himself. His participation in the type of political corruption which he so much deplored was too much for him to admit. It surprised no one when the frustrated and distraught Borden submitted his resignation to the Conservative caucus early in 1905. But the caucus had no alternative to Borden; it forgave him for losing the election, forgot the Graham fiasco, and begged him to remain as leader. After brief hesitation, Borden agreed. Having made the decision, he began to take a more logical and thorough approach to political leadership. He extended his attempts to lure better men into political life, especially from the business world where he believed that the most talented men of the age were found. He also gave up his law practice and his Halifax home, selecting as his new residence a splendid mansion on Wurtemburg Street overlooking Ottawa's Rideau River. Nine years after Borden entered the House of Commons, four years after he became Conservative leader, politics finally became his full-time profession.

Unlike law, diligence, intelligence and commitment were not sufficient to assure success in politics. Borden's major obstacle to political success sat opposite him in the House of Commons: the leader of the Liberal Party, Prime Minister Sir Wilfrid Laurier. A politician whom we would now call charismatic, Laurier dominated Canadian politics and his times. He possessed in abundance those gifts of eloquence and personal magnetism which Borden so obviously lacked. With

*Full details on the plot may be found in R. C. Brown, *Robert Laird Borden, A Biography, Vol. 1, 1854-1914* (Toronto, Macmillan, 1975), Chapter 5.

a prosperous nation behind it, Laurier's government seemed an impregnable bastion to the opposition. While Borden's Conservatives plodded well-prepared into political battle, Laurier's counterattack invariably confounded his opponents with its inspired brilliance.

Borden and his colleagues did expose the glaring weaknesses of the Laurier government: its corruption, its internal divisions, its indecisiveness, and its lack of program, but they could not undermine popular support for Wilfrid Laurier. Borden came to the conclusion that he could win only if issues rather than personalities captured the attention of the Canadian people. In 1907, therefore, he presented a remarkably progressive platform, the so-called "Halifax platform," which contrasted sharply with the nebulous Liberal program of the time. In this policy statement, Borden called for such reforms as civil service appointments through examination, the end of corrupt electoral politics, public ownership of telegraphs and telephones, senate reform, and free rural mail delivery. Within a year, Borden had won a most important, though from the Tory point of view, rather unfortunate convert to many of these ideas — Sir Wilfrid Laurier. By 1908, Laurier had placed much of Borden's program on the statute books. Outflanked once again by his clever adversary, Borden and his Conservatives endured their fourth successive defeat in the general election of 1908.

What were the Conservatives to do against this gifted

An early motorcade in the election campaign of 1911. Notice that the expensive cars, carrying the notables, come first. The Model-T Fords come along behind.

but, in Borden's eyes, superficial Liberal government? Many Conservatives had a straightforward answer: get a new leader. The major complaint against Borden was that he was "a lovely fellow," but, as Sam Hughes put it, he lacked "political guts." Borden on the hustings was too much like Borden in the courtroom, trying to win through the rationality and common sense of his argument. In the House of Commons also, he lacked the instincts of a political infighter. In each year after 1908, disillusioned Tories challenged his leadership, and Borden was fortunate that they did. To the surprise of his opponents, his allies, and probably even himself, he overcame each challenge and in doing so gained a new confidence and understanding of Canadian politics.

A political novice seeks out new political worlds to conquer; a practised politician builds on strength. After 1908, Borden became a practised politician. Even before the 1908 debacle, Borden had begun to appreciate that he should worry less about the Conservatives' weak flanks and concentrate more upon the strengthening of the Conservative bastions of British Columbia, Manitoba and Ontario. These three provinces shared a "British" outlook, Conservative governments with large majorities, and a willingness to support the Federal Tories. Borden therefore carefully cultivated close ties with the premiers of these provinces, men who seemed to him to possess a progressive outlook not found among the Tories in Ottawa. With the aid of these premiers, Borden withstood the assault upon his leadership, built an organization superior to that of the Laurier government, and developed a new program which united his fractured party.

It must be admitted that this new program, whose core was acceptance of Imperial responsibility, owed more to accident than to deliberation. Since the end of the Boer War, the Imperialist fires in Canada had been rarely stoked. After 1907, however, more Canadians became aware of and concerned about the new threat to the Empire posed by the rise of the German Navy, and many English Canadians advocated support for the British in this crisis. All Canadian politicians realized the highly inflammable content of such an issue and most sought to moderate its intensity, but Sir George Foster, who possessed, in Borden's words, "the political sense of a turnip," did not share this tendency. In the early spring of 1909, Foster, over the strident opposition of his Quebec Conservative colleagues, moved a resolution imploring Canada to assume the burden of defence of her coasts. Borden and

OPPOSITE
Henri Bourassa, the eloquent and fiery French-Canadian nationalist. Founder of *Le Devoir*, still a highly influential newspaper in Quebec.

62

Laurier meeting with government leaders in 1913: (left to right) Hon. Martin Burrell, Minister of Agriculture; Hon. Thomas White, Minister of Finance; Prime Minister Borden; Sir Wilfrid Laurier; Hon. George Foster, Minister of Trade and Commerce.
Public Archives Canada, PA-51531.

Laurier, sensing the acute danger involved, moved to smother the resolution in ambiguity and apparent unanimous compromise. They did not succeed.

Soon many of the most powerful Conservatives in English Canada, including the provincial premiers Whitney of Ontario, McBride of British Columbia, and Roblin of Manitoba, denounced the Conservative Parliamentarians for so readily agreeing to Laurier's shrewd compromise and for missing the opportunity to show solidarity with the mother country in time of danger. On the other hand, Laurier's former colleague, the French Canadian nationalist, Henri Bourassa, quickly turned his attention from provincial to federal politics and denounced the Laurier Naval Bill, which envisaged the building of a Canadian navy, as a pernicious manoeuvre designed to draw Canada into the vortex of European militarism.

The naval debate threatened both parties, but by late 1910 it was clear that the Liberals' position was the more difficult. Laurier described his dilemma well: "I am branded in Quebec as a traitor to the French and in Ontario as a traitor to the English. . . . In Quebec I am attacked as an Imperialist, and in Ontario as an anti-Imperialist." Many English Canadian Liberals who were Imperialists and who were also disillusioned with Laurier's reluctance to implement a reform program, started to move towards political independence. But it was in Quebec that the first tangible evidence of Laurier's troubles was manifested. In a November 1910 by-election in Drummond-Arthabaska constituency, where Laurier himself had once practised law, the anti-Government candidate, who had been strongly supported by the nationalist Bourassa and the Quebec Conservative leader, Frederick Monk unexpectedly triumphed.

So startling was this upset that many Conservatives believed they had already plucked the flower of victory from among the many nettles surrounding the naval question. But Laurier had not yet exhausted his bag of political tricks. Early in the new year, Finance Minister Fielding presented a reciprocity agreement with the United States to the House of Commons. The Conservatives were shocked: Foster declared that his heart sank into his boots as Fielding spoke; other Tories uttered prophecies of political doom for their party. Borden, however, would have none of this. To him, reciprocity would tie Canada inextricably to the United States and make her a pale reflection of the southern nation's undoubted majesty. She would be just another hinterland, another North Dakota. Borden's tone and his argument struck a responsible chord among central Canadian businessmen whose industries had extended their web over the Canadian East and West and among Imperialists whose grandiose vision of Canadian paramountcy within the Empire was threatened by reciprocity. Soon, many raised their voices against it and for the Conservative opposition. Borden was doubly heartened, first by the reversal of the defeatist tide which had initially overwhelmed the Tory M.P.'s, and secondly, by the excellence of the converts to his cause. Into the Tory camp came men like Thomas White, a widely admired Toronto businessman, Sir Edmund Walker, President of the Bank of Commerce, and Clifford Sifton, the best minister in the early Laurier governments. With such men, one could build a truly great party. But not all agreed.

The party regulars rebelled against the newcomers' influence in the spring of 1911, but Borden stood firm and endured with the help of the increasingly powerful Conservative provincial premiers. Laurier misjudged Borden's internal party problems and thinking that the Tory party seethed with dissension, he called an election for September 21. Borden was delighted. Fortified by the newcomers and by the wholehearted support of the Tory provincial premiers,

he prepared to meet the test, more optimistic than ever before. The Conservative campaign of 1911 has often been described as negative, and in Quebec, where Bourassa and Borden made a covert alliance, it surely was. The irony of the anti-Imperialist Bourassa carrying the Tory banner was not lost on Liberals of the time or on the historians in the future. Also, economic historians have largely agreed that the 1911 reciprocity bargain was a good one for Canada and that reciprocity would have rationalized the economic life of the North American continent.

But Borden's arguments in 1911 were not economic, not even rational in the strict sense. Leaving Quebec in the hands of Bourassa and Monk, he stirred the emotions of the English Canadian, appealing to his British blood and to his vision of a strong, independent Canada. "I believe," Borden warned in his final campaign address,

> that we are ... standing today at the parting of the ways. ... We must decide whether the spirit of Canadianism or of Continentalism shall prevail on the northern half of this continent. ... With Canada's youthful vitality, her rapidly increasing population, her marvellous material resources, her spirit of hopefulness and energy, she can place herself within a comparatively brief period in the highest position within this mighty Empire. This is the path upon which we have proceeded — this is the path from which we are asked to depart ...

This dream was a mirage; the Imperial path was soon to narrow and eventually came to an end. But in 1911, English Canadians chose to follow Robert Borden on the familiar path whence they had proceeded. Faithful to his past and conscious of his burden, Robert Borden became the eighth prime minister of Canada on October 15, 1911.

3
The New Conservative Party, 1911-1914

THE CONSERVATIVE VICTORY in 1911 was coincident with the twilight of the great Canadian boom. The seemingly inexhaustible Northwest had begun to notice and to assess its new burdens; cities swollen by waves of newcomers encountered baffling problems of slums, poverty, and even pollution; and businessmen started to reject the unrestricted competition of the boom years in favour of protection of their gains. The appointment of a Commission of Conservation in 1909 signified that the nation knew that it must take stock, measure its accomplishments and plan its future. The pell-mell prosperity of the first decade of the century had carried Canadians far beyond the boundaries of the old charts. The task of creating new ones fell upon Canada's leaders, particularly her new prime minister, Robert Laird Borden. In many ways, Laurier was fortunate that he lost the election. His legacy to Borden included several important and difficult problems: a boom that was running its course, a massive influx of immi-

Borden and his cabinet at Government House on October 10, 1911, just after the ministers had been sworn in. The ceremony was the last official act of Earl Grey, the retiring Governor General. From left to right are: The Hon. Sam Hughes, the Hon. R. Rogers, the Hon. J. D. Reid, the Hon. C. J. Doherty, the Hon. W. J. Roche, the Hon. George E. Foster, the Hon. J. D. Hazen, the Hon. R. L. Borden, the Hon. L. P. Pelletier, the Hon. T. W. Crothers, the Hon. A. E. Kemp, the Hon. George H. Perley, the Hon. Senator James Lougheed, the Hon. Frank Cochrane, the Hon. Bruno Nantel, the Hon. F. D. Monk, and the Hon. W. T. White. *Public Archives Canada, C-23913.*

grants, railway financial troubles and a deteriorating international situation.

Within a year of Borden's victory, the first signs of recession appeared, and after more than a decade of uninterrupted growth, the impact of the economic slowdown was especially marked. Moreover, the hundreds of thousands of immigrants that Laurier had brought to Canada were no longer seen as a valuable addition to a scarce labour supply but rather as the major cause of Canadian unemployment. Nor could the open door be immediately closed: in 1912, 375,000 newcomers arrived in Canada and in 1913, when recession became depression, a record 400,000 immigrants made Canada their new home. Canada's welcome was not especially friendly; indeed, in some cases, it was openly hostile. In May 1914, when the *Komagata Maru* entered Vancouver harbour with 376 East Indians aboard, the local officials refused to allow it to land. While hysteria reigned in many British Columbian quarters, the Canadian government ordered its cruiser *Rainbow* to drive the unwanted intruder out of the Canadian waters. The East Indians returned home, but many others, especially Orientals, who were allowed to stay found their new surroundings distinctly unpleasant and many of their fellow Canadians, overtly racist.

The railways had thrived upon the immigrant hordes, recruiting them in Europe, bringing them on their ships and then transporting them to their new homes in Ontario or the West. When it seemed that growth was perpetual, railways were the favourite of investors and governments. So boundless was Laurier's faith in the railways and Canada's future that he permitted two new railways to be built across the West, the Grand Trunk Pacific and the Canadian Northern. Both were supported by federal and provincial governments through liberal bond guarantees. It was very easy to be generous when it seemed the guarantees were unlikely ever to have financial effects. But by 1913 when the lustre of Canadian prosperity had faded, these guarantees promised to undermine the financial fabric of Canadian federalism.

There was very little any Canadian government could have done to end depression, to heal racial conflict or to ensure European peace. Borden's naval proposals were at least an attempt to bolster British strength, to Borden's mind the best assurance of European peace. But in this as in other measures intended to deal with domestic problems, he faced a strong antagonist in the partisan Liberal Senate. As Borden realized

OPPOSITE
Sir Sam Hughes, Minister of Militia and Defence during the first two years of the war. His lack of tact and discretion made him a difficult colleague, and Borden had to ask for his resignation in November 1916.
Public Archives Canada, C-20240.

71

Robert Rogers, one of the more colourful members of Borden's first cabinet. *Public Archives Canada, C-52197.*

the seriousness of his predicament, he tended to blame Laurier for artfully concealing inefficiency and clumsiness beneath the facade of competence. Laurier, of course, would not accept the blame. The result was a deeper hostility between the two parties which made successful government even more difficult to achieve.

All of Borden's problems were not of Laurier's making. He had not attracted sufficient talent to Conservative ranks to create a first rate cabinet. Moreover, in the quest for power, he had made promises and alliances which were sure to be potentially embarrassing. All this became apparent as he performed the delicate balancing act required when forming a Canadian cabinet. Borden later recalled that he had to endure "excursions and alarums" by Conservatives from all parts of the country. Foster, a rejected suitor for the portfolio of Minister of Finance, echoed Borden's complaints about the pro-

cess: "More people — more wirepulling, deputations galore and general suspense."

The greatest suspense arose from two major problems which confronted Borden. First, what should be done about the Quebec Nationalists who had helped so much in the campaign but who would be most troublesome in the cabinet? While Borden wanted to consolidate the Conservative gains in Quebec, he could not risk offending the Imperialists, a bulwark of the Conservative Party in English Canada. Secondly, how should the Liberals and independents who had spoken out against reciprocity and for Borden be rewarded? In this case, Borden himself was eager to choose a cabinet minister from the Liberal rebel ranks, but he knew that his choice, no matter how competent or non-partisan, would meet with strong objection from the die-hard Tories. And of course to these unusual considerations were added the old ones of balancing

Sir George Foster, Borden's Minister of Trade and Commerce. The most durable of ministers, he served in the cabinets of no fewer than seven prime ministers: Macdonald, Abbott, Thompson, Bowell, Tupper, Borden and Meighen.
Public Archives Canada, C-4078.

PARIS COMES TO YOU THIS SPRING

reversing the former order of things through which you had to go to Paris, for we have here presented—through our buying office situated in the heart of that world of fashion—a glimpse of what is being worn to-day in the gay capital. These dress styles (and the Waists on page 32) are from some of the most celebrated Paris designers, and are shown here in order to afford our patrons an opportunity of purchasing styles which have not been altered in any way, but are offered just as they came from the original French modellers.

"My gown was made by a Paris costumier" may now be the expression of the woman who has the desire to say so.

These Dresses were personally selected by fashion experts at our Paris office, and the goods faithfully sketched by French artists.

PARIS MODEL 56-177
designed in Liberty Satin ("Charmante"), tailored bodice in surplice effect, lined with silk, and featuring the latest Parisian under-shoulder draped sleeve, also the trouserine hip style with coat formation at the back. Collar, revers and cuffs of white silk voile, edged with open-work trimming. Bust sizes 34, 36, 38 and 40. Skirt length 40 inches (deep hem). Colors Navy, Grey, Copenhagen, Mahogany or Black.
Price **35.00**

PARIS MODEL 56-176
developed in White Cotton Crepon, lined throughout with mercerized mull; the little colored waistcoat and lower hip frill embroidered in white Ratine effect, while the guimpe and revers, also the cuff points, are of fine silk crepon in the new shades. An Oriental embroidered plastron trims the back of the waist. Bust sizes 34, 36, 38 or 40. Skirt length 40 inches (deep hem). White only, with choice of trimmings in Nattier Blue and Apricot, Rose and Canary, or Tan and Nattier Blue.
Price **25.00**

PARIS MODEL 56-178
is of plain Liberty Satin ("Regence"). The bodice, which is silk-lined, has a waistcoat of tulle finished with a ruche, the collar covered with fine guipure lace, while the sleeves are of the latest under-arm droop style. The skirt has the new fluffy panier, and closely pleated flounce all around; deep girdle of self. Bust sizes 34, 36, 38 or 40. Skirt length 40 inches (deep hem). Colors Nattier Blue, Tan, Rose, Navy or Black. Price... **30.00**

PARIS MODEL 56-179
of White Cotton Crepon, with the bodice part and the three frills (which fall over the back of the skirt) in colored stripe crepon, while each side of the full-length front panel is hem-stitch-finished. The self-fringed sash is of vari-colored silk in the popular Bayadere stripe. Bust sizes 34, 36, 38 or 40. Skirt length 40 inches (deep hem). White only, with choice of trimming in Navy, Old Rose or Straw shade.
Price **16.50**

DIRECT FROM PARIS TO YOU, MADAM

To those who purchase from these "Foretastes of Fashion" we would say the styles are by no means extreme, nor were they selected with this idea in view, but are carefully chosen as representative of good taste and utility, at the same time extending the range of selections in Dress Models as given on pages 18 to 20. A limited number only of each style has been imported, so that orders should reach us early to prevent disappointment.

PARIS MODEL 56-175
showing the new triple Cascade drape in an exquisite weave of Colored Silk Crepon, with white polka dots, lined throughout with silk. The guimpe and cuffs are of spotted net; fichu collar and cuff bands of embroidered chiffon and pleated tulle. Sash of satin charmeuse, with silk acorn tassel finish. Bust sizes 34, 36, 38 or 40. Skirt length 40 inches (deep hem). Colors Apricot, Tango, Marine Blue or Violet. Price. **35.00**

Models "direct from Paris" advertised by Eaton's
in the summer of 1914.
Archives, Eaton's of Canada Limited.

Closing of Parliament in 1914.
Public Archives Canada, PA-23307.

Catholic and Protestant, Easterner and Westerner, and party service and competence.

In the end, the new cabinet was a colourful pastiche of Quebec Nationalist, British Imperialist, and political bagman. Some stood out above the others: Robert Rogers, the "Honourable Bob" to his many friends, whose skills at political manipulation – Liberals called it political skulduggery – was already legendary; Sam Hughes, a political Baron Munchausen, full of wild tales of martial exploits and lurid intrigues; and Frank Cochrane, a former provincial politician in Ontario,

On the evening of February 3, 1916, fire swept through the centre block of the Parliament Buildings. This photograph was taken the next morning. Like most great fires, this one was somewhat freakish in what it destroyed and what it spared. Laurier's office, containing all his papers

whose remarkable business success on the frontier of Ontario endowed him with an inveterate optimism and a laconic arrogance. Foster, an eloquent temperance lecturer when he was discovered by John A. Macdonald, who undoubtedly thought it a shame to waste such talent on such a poor cause, became Minister of Trade and Commerce. The fact that Foster had defrauded Borden on some mining stocks was only one of several factors which made Foster's own preference, Finance, inappropriate for him. The Finance portfolio therefore went to the Toronto businessman Thomas White, a Liberal until 1911, and who, like most recent proselytes, had not yet won the trust, much less the affection of his new colleagues. There were a few others who deserve special mention. Jack "Doc" Reid, an Eastern Ontario physician, and Thomas Crothers were both competent administrators. Their membership in the cabinet is interesting, however, because less than a year earlier they were leaders in the rebellion against Borden. The inclusion of another rebel, Frederick Monk, is more understandable. Unfortunately, Monk's congenital nervousness, a handicap to any politician, was heightened by his crucial position as the liaison between Borden and the Nationalists of Quebec.

As one might expect in the case of a party long out of power, the new Conservative cabinet was worried about their performance in the first session of the new parliament. But the Liberals were not in a mood to grant the new government a honeymoon, not even a brief one. The defeat had irritated Laurier and his party; the Conservative-Nationalist alliance had infuriated them. Moreover, the Liberals knew that political office would quickly dispel the mists which had shrouded the Conservative naval policy before 1911 and would reveal the contradictions and the deception in that policy. The Liberals also believed that the naval question would almost certainly divide the Tory Party and perhaps even cause the fall of the government. For that reason above all others, the Liberals moved immediately to the attack.

Although naval policy was fraught with danger, Borden, for personal and political reasons, accepted that it must be the first and the major priority of the new government. In March 1912, Laurier's naval program of 1910 was scuttled. But how could Borden frame a new policy which offended neither the Nationalist nor the Imperialist on his party's benches? Refusing to commit himself publicly, although privately accepting the need for an "emergency contribution,"

for the years 1912-15, was completely burned out; the room next door suffered only a small singed spot on one wall. *Public Archives Canada, PA-9249.*

Four disasters of the most diverse kind marked the Borden years in Canada: the Regina tornado of 1912, the burning of the Parliament Buildings and the collapse of the Quebec Bridge in 1916, and the Halifax explosion of 1917. At Quebec, in September 1916, as the centre span of the great cantilever bridge the spans the St. Lawrence was being hoisted into place, a support gave way and the span fell into the river. A replacement was safely installed the next year.
Copyright: Chesterfield & McLaren.
Public Archives Canada, C-57787.

Borden embarked for Britain in June 1912 to determine how serious the European emergency was. Not surprisingly, the British said that it was very serious indeed and that a cash contribution from Canada for the construction of warships was therefore essential. The First Lord of the Admiralty, Winston Churchill, already a political master, privately told Borden that he was "quite willing to play the game" by giving a statement in writing urging the necessity of an emergency contribution from Canada. This was a game that Borden, too, was willing to play. He sailed for Canada convinced that the English Liberal, Churchill, had handed him a trump card to defeat the Canadian Liberals.

He was soon disillusioned. In cabinet, Monk refused to believe that Churchill's messages constituted *prima facie* evidence of an emergency. Borden, Monk argued, must present his case to the Canadian people as he had promised to do before the election. On the other hand, the English Canadian ministers almost unanimously opposed a plebiscite which they believed would indicate weakness and indecision. The Conservatives had been given a mandate; now they must carry it out.

Regina's almost forgotten ordeal: a general view of the city after the tornado of June 30, 1912. It lasted only a few minutes, but it destroyed 500 buildings, took 30 lives and left 2500 people homeless.
Archives of Saskatchewan.

Borden agreed. On October 18, 1912, less than a year after assuming office, Monk resigned, stating that he could not abandon *his* campaign pledge whatever the rest of the cabinet might do. With Monk gone and most of the remaining French Canadian Conservatives subdued through various means of coercion, the naval proposals appeared to have clear sailing ahead. Accordingly, on December 5, 1912, Borden presented a Naval Aid Bill which called for a $35,000,000 contribution to the British Navy. The Conservative clamour during

Overturned vehicles and smashed buildings dotted the rubble left by the tornado.
Archives of Saskatchewan.

On December 6, 1917, a munitions ship exploded in Halifax Harbour, devastating a square mile of the city and taking 1630 lives.
Public Archives Canada, C-19945.

Borden's speech and the singing of "Rule Britannia" at its end intensified the Liberals' anger and hence their opposition.

Borden had naïvely thought that popular Imperialist sentiment would compel many English-Canadian Liberals to support his naval bill. He did not reckon with Laurier's hold over his supporters, with the English-Canadian Liberals' reluctance to play the Churchill-Borden game, and with the determination and persistence of Sir Wilfrid Laurier on this one issue. The Liberals debated and argued, endlessly it seemed. It was February 27 before the Bill passed second reading in the House. Still the debate dragged on, long into the evenings and weekends. Borden's confidence ebbed and his frustration mounted with unfortunate physical consequences: boils. Members on both sides worked "shifts" as the House debated through the night. Finally, he could stand no more. On April 9, 1913, four months after the beginning of the naval debate, Borden — probably a comic sight with his neck swathed in bandages to cover his boils — introduced a motion for closure, a motion which would deny the Liberals the right to continue the debate. With closure the bill soon passed, but Borden's

victory was short-lived. The Senate, which was dominated by Liberals, rejected Borden's cherished naval bill and dared the Prime Minister to submit the policy to the Canadian people. That was a challenge which Borden could not accept. When war came, there was neither a Canadian Navy nor three dreadnoughts in the Royal Navy contributed by Canada. In a tragic way, however, Borden had been vindicated; the emergency had been real.

So it was with much of Borden's legislative program; its value is clear to the historian but it was not so obvious to contemporaries. Under Borden, the Conservatives began a genuine attempt to come to grips with the new industrial and urban Canada. Three principal factors acted to frustrate this effort: administrative incompetence, public indifference, and Senatorial obstruction. The federal bureaucracy which Borden inherited was totally unsuited to the needs of a modern state. He and his cabinet met six days a week, not because so many matters of national import demanded attention, but because the cabinet had to consider the essentially trivial business of patronage. Laurier's establishment of a Civil Service Commission in 1908 had helped very little. The Commission appointed only the inner civil service; the system of recruitment for the "outside" civil service remained political patronage and Borden knew that extension of the merit principle beyond Ottawa would meet with strong resistance from within his own party.

Telephone lines were beginning to tie together the country of Borden's era, though conditions were still somewhat primitive. Exchanges were often set up in places of business, or even in private homes. Here an operator perches on his stool in the corner of Dr. Riddell's drugstore, Lauder, Manitoba.
Public Archives Canada, PA-70872.

Tories like Sam Hughes and Bob Rogers viewed abolition of patronage as tantamount to political suicide, and they were not completely wrong. To "clean up" the civil service would require strong public backing. There was support in the universities, in the churches, and, for that matter, in the civil service itself, which was often appalled by the appointment of incompetent political partisans to highly important positions. But in 1911 most Canadians were too absorbed in building new homes, seeking new opportunities and making fortunes, large and small, to give much thought to civil service reform. Frankly, it was not an idea that won the hearts of many men. As a result, civil service reform continued to take place in a piecemeal fashion.

The same public indifference that delayed civil service reform permitted the Liberal Senate to defeat not only Borden's naval bill but also his highways bill and his tariff commission bill. These last two were important components of the progressive program outlined by Borden during the election campaign. There were not yet many automobiles in Canada — about 50,000 in 1913, according to one estimate — but their future importance was obvious. The highways bill

OPPOSITE
Robert Borden in Windsor uniform.
Public Archives Canada, C-22567.

BELOW
Electric automobiles, which were in their heyday in the last years before the First World War, were considered the ideal personal car for the well-to-do woman of fashion. This Tate electric was built in Walkerville. It was unusual in that it offered a roadster model, with the male motorist in mind, as well as the usual coupe.
Canada on Wheels.
Oberon Press.

"Trees," Homer Watson
wrote, "are the first of all
the beauties with which
the Lord has embroidered
this old earth." He painted
this picture, entitled
Evening After Rain, in
1913. Watson was one of
the first painters to make
Canadians conscious of the
special qualities of their
own landscapes, but his
technique was quite
different from that of the
Group of Seven, whose
broader treatment did not
appeal to him.
Art Gallery of Ontario.

David Milne's approach to painting was highly personal. Like every artist he had been subject to influences, notably Fauvism, but his work became quite distinctive and quite different from that of his Canadian contemporaries. *The Blue Rocker*, for which his wife was the model, was painted in 1914.
Art Gallery of Ontario.

Vancouver in 1912.
Vancouver City Archives.

would have provided the financial catalyst for the construction of a network of roads which would bring Canada's isolated communities closer together, both economically and culturally. The tariff commission bill envisaged the formation of a commission which would "scientifically" regulate the tariff and thereby take that contentious subject out of the hands of the "unscientific" politicians. For no good reason, the Senate struck down both bills, leaving Canada without federal support for highway construction until 1919 and without a coherent and logical tariff policy until the end of the war. In Great Britain, where an intransigent House of Lords blocked a Liberal government's program, the government went to the country and won a resounding vote of confidence which forced the upper chamber to desist. Alas, Borden had no such option for the boom had ended and an election was inconceivable in such circumstances.

Borden and his Finance Minister, Thomas White, quickly diagnosed the malady; but, unfortunately, they did not know the medicine for the economic ills. White's choice of remedy, a reduction in government expenditure, only worsened the problems, although White could not have understood this at the time. Because Canadians had not expected a depression, they were most unprepared for it when it came. The industrialization and urbanization of the past two decades also worked to intensify personal hardship. The new city dweller often lacked the financial assistance of friends or the plot of land that would produce the food to sustain him and his family

Regina in 1913, seen from the Parliament Buildings, with Wascana Lake in the foreground. This photograph was taken only fourteen months after the tornado of 1912 and shows the astonishing way in which the city recovered from the disaster.
Archives of Saskatchewan.

through the long Canadian winter. Nor were the cities prepared for the demands for help from the unemployed. As small towns grew into cities, commitments to new industries, transportation projects and all kinds of other capital expenditures used up most of the slender revenues from taxation. When depression came, there was little left for the unemployed and the newcomer. Social reformers and clergymen tried to fill the vacuum with city missions and settlement houses which would serve the material and spiritual needs of the indigent. Such efforts were admirable but they were also quite inadequate.

While relief for the unemployed had always been a local responsibility, relief for Canada's perpetually impoverished railways was, to Borden's dismay, a federal responsibility, practically if not constitutionally. Very soon after the economic downturn, William Mackenzie and his partner, Donald Mann, of the Canadian Northern Railway came to Borden's office pleading for special aid to complete their transcontinental railway. To make matters worse, the Grand Trunk syndicate also requested a government loan of fifteen million dollars to complete their unnecessary railway. There were so many better things on which the government could spend public funds. Moreover, these two railways which had so long supported the Laurier government seemed like brazen political harlots, now promising favours to the new Borden government in return for financial support. Borden fumed, the cabinet grumbled, but there was little that they could do. Borden had talked earlier of public ownership but the idea had attracted little support from his caucus and from the public. Accordingly, nationalization was not considered at this time. Yet to deny the railways their demands would probably cause them to default on their obligations, an unthinkable prospect to politicians of the day. The railways, too, had become the symbol of Canada's growth and her hopes for future greatness. The subsidy and loans were therefore granted, and Canada's most expensive and popular public sport, railway building, continued.

And there were other problems within the party. Borden's refusal to purge the public service was taken as a personal affront by many of his colleagues. Conservatives in the constituencies whose election night enthusiasm could often be explained by visions of political plums dancing before their eyes deluged Ottawa with complaints. Sam Hughes warned Borden that the Conservatives were "getting it in the neck" wherever they neglected to throw the Grits out of their civil

Winnipeg in 1914.
Public Archives Canada,
PA-10991.

service sinecures. But Borden would not budge. During the campaign, he had promised that only "offensive partisanship" would be adequate grounds for dismissal. Furthermore, Borden believed that he had more important things to worry about: the imperial question, the economic troubles and several other matters of national concern. Why should the Prime Minister of Canada have to become involved in the appointment of the janitor at the Halifax Post Office? The answer soon became clear. As the Prime Minister withdrew almost entirely from party activities, various ministers built up their own personal fiefdoms. The result was little coordination, ministerial disagreements, and an infuriating uncertainty for the party rank and file. With the party leader shunning his

traditional, if unpleasant, party task, the powerful Conservative machine of 1911 fell into a state of serious disrepair.

The consequences of Borden's aversion to party work were greatest in Quebec. After Monk refused to support the naval bill, Borden tended to ignore Quebec, expecting that in good time the French Canadians would see the foolishness of their actions. He had no close French Canadian friends, nor did he appear to want to cultivate any. It is fair to suggest, as Professor Craig Brown has done, that Borden was indifferent to French Canada and that he believed national development must take pre-eminence over any special claims it might put

Next to the war, railways were the most serious problem with which Borden had to deal. It arose largely from the ambitions of three men — Sir William Mackenzie, Sir Donald Mann and Charles M. Hays. Mackenzie (opposite) and Mann (above) built the Canadian Northern; Hays was responsible for

the Grand Trunk Pacific. Mackenzie and Mann were knighted in 1911, shortly before the end of the boom that had enabled them to float their grandiose enterprise. Hays was drowned when the *Titanic* sank in 1912, and did not live to see the collapse of the Grand Trunk.
Public Archives Canada, C-23691 and C-6653.

forward. It seemed to him that French Canada had not yet achieved political maturity; and, for Borden, no better evidence of this existed than his own French-Canadian colleagues. They were a burden that a political leader must bear until the "coming of age" of Quebec finally took place. Quebec was a province unlike the others; it was almost completely ignored by Borden. Thomas Chase Casgrain, a veteran Conservative politician, could complain to his leader:

There is nothing doing here; no organization; no stirring up of the masses; no educational campaign; no telling our people what we have done, what we intend doing; nothing to inspire the young men with confidence in the future of the Conservative Party.

But the complaints were not heeded, and by 1914 the future of the Conservative Party in Quebec seemed very bleak indeed.

The three years after 1911 had not been easy ones for Borden. The enthusiasm of his followers had dissipated; his legislative program had not found its place in the Statutes of Canada. Most disappointing, surely, was the fate of the naval bill. Through the contribution to Britain, Borden had hoped to purchase not merely military security for Canada and the Empire but also a voice in the making of Imperial foreign policy. In common with most Imperialists, he believed that such a role would be a major step towards national maturity. And it was through the acceptance of international and imperial responsibility that Canadians would dispel the narrow-mindedness, materialism, and parochialism that had marked them in the past.

Borden never lost this belief, though the method of its fulfillment became less certain. As his domestic program languished and his faith in the effectiveness of the political system waned, he continued to work and hope for a master stroke which would leave a lasting stamp of his tenure upon his nation. Unlike most Canadians, Borden saw that modernization, for all its benefits, had brought serious problems which were far beyond the capacity of the existing rudimentary state machinery to solve. There were no simple panaceas, only hard work and time. Not surprisingly, Borden came to see himself primarily as an educator, one who would show Canadians that each one of them "owes a duty to the state as sacred as that which he owes to his family or to his neighbours." Canadians must learn, Borden argued, to overlook "mere transient, temporary and local considerations," for, in truth, "the interest of the East is the interest of the West, the interest of Nova Scotia is and always must be the interest of British Columbia as well." The Canadian people proved to be poor students in this lesson.

Nevertheless, there were personal satisfactions which derived from public duty, and Borden's 1912 journey to England was undoubtedly the principal one. The public portion of the trip was spent in difficult and often unsuccessful negotiations on the naval question. Far more fascinating to Borden was his encounter with the brilliance and elegance of Edwardian England. Before World War I, the British aristocracy ex-

OPPOSITE
Borden with Winston Churchill, then First Lord of the Admiralty, in London in the summer of 1912. Their discussions prompted the introduction of Borden's ill-fated Naval Aid Bill late in the year. *Public Archives Canada,* C-2082.

An unusual profile photograph of Sir Robert Borden, taken in 1918. Unless they are working from living subjects, sculptors often find it difficult to determine the shape of a person's head. This picture was of considerable assistance to Frances Loring when she was working on the Borden statue for Parliament Hill. She once remarked: "Any Canadian who is in the least danger of becoming celebrated should be photographed from behind as well as from in front!" *Public Archives Canada, C-8107.*

cited Canadian imaginations as Hollywood was to do in later decades. Not surprisingly, the Grand Pré farmboy who had become Canada's prime minister was captivated by the grand country homes, the conversation and even the arrogance of upper-class English life. How daring, yet how flattering it was when Nancy Astor telephoned the King, inviting His Majesty to spend the weekend with her guests, the Bordens, at Cliveden! Perhaps the Astors were dull people – the King almost certainly was – but the associations, the history, and the style combined to create an atmosphere which intoxicated the Canadian visitor. That for Canadians was part of being British. And there was more.

For most English Canadians, especially those of the middle

OPPOSITE
Mrs. Borden.
Public Archives Canada, C-5654.

Children's toys advertised with Christmas 1914 in mind. Price levels at the time are well illustrated by the complete mechanical train offered for 35 cents. *Archives, Eaton's of Canada Limited.*

class, being British made them a part of a great human enterprise and gave them a history stretching far beyond the brief interlude and ambit of their own land. In Kipling's tales of faraway corners of the Empire, young Canadians could feel they had a place. In the libraries of the Rosedale and Westmount mansions, which mirrored in every detail the best and worst of British architecture, the English classics were prominently displayed, as they were in more modest bindings in humbler homes. Borden and most English Canadians considered themselves British just as much as the Yorkshireman. Because this sense of Britishness lurked so deeply in Borden's soul, there was no doubt that he would defend the British Empire with all the power he could muster. His opportunity would come very soon.

Laura Borden captures her husband at golf in this photo she took at Glensmere in 1913. *Public Archives Canada, C-21314.*

4
The Impact of War

Troops entraining at St. Thomas, Ontario, on their way to embarkation port and service overseas: a poignant scene enacted many times in cities all across Canada.
Public Archives Canada, PA-22759.

Eager recruits forcing their way into the recruiting centre in Ottawa in the first days of the First World War. No one had any conception of what lay ahead; the chief anxiety of many was fear that the war would be over before they had a chance to participate in it.
Canadian War Museum, National Museum of Man, National Museums Canada.

BECAUSE CANADA WAS A BRITISH NATION in August 1914, she went to war. There was no hesitation, no public dissent, simply a recognition that Canada must share the Imperial burden. In those first early days, no Canadian expressed this view more eloquently than Sir Wilfrid Laurier whose forceful words quickly subdued scattered French-Canadian Liberal opposition to Canadian participation in Europe's conflict. The war, Sir Wilfrid declared, was to be fought by and for Britain and France, "the noblest expressions" of "highest civilization." Because of the gravity of the impending struggle, Laurier pledged that he would "raise no question, . . . take no exception, . . . offer no criticism, so long as there is danger at the front." By the fervour of these words in August 1914, Laurier hoped he would eradicate any grounds for suspicion of his loyalty in English Canada and would persuade French Canadians that their English-Canadian countrymen regarded the conflict with great seriousness. Unlike many Canadians, Laurier knew that the real threat to Canada lay not in Europe but on the boundaries of English and French Canada. The passions of war would greatly magnify the tensions of peace-time. Compromise and understanding were therefore essential; Canada must not become a country divided by war. To maintain unity in wartime was to be the most difficult and important task of Laurier's long career.

Initially, the war did not interrupt the daily lives of most Canadians. It was mainly the unemployed, the British immigrant and the chronic adventurer who rushed to the recruiting offices. Almost immediately the new recruits departed for Valcartier Camp near Quebec City where Sam Hughes was training or, perhaps more accurately, attempting to train the first Canadian Division. The flamboyant Hughes, terrified lest the war end before the Canadian troops arrived in Europe, had dispensed with his own Department of Militia's mobilization scheme. Within a few weeks Hughes and some more competent aides had fashioned a military camp for over thirty thousand men complete with a castle topped by a flag in which Sam himself dwelt. Strutting up and down the ranks, barking out orders which he countermanded within minutes, and spinning long tales of his own martial exploits, Hughes was a bundle of comic energy and incredible conceit. Although Hughes basked in the public acclaim for the "miracle at

In the first month of the war a battalion was raised and named Princess Patricia's Canadian Light Infantry, in honour of the daughter of the Duke of Connaught, the Governor General. The Princess is shown here with officers of the battalion at Bramshott, one of the Canadian Army camps in England.
Public Archives Canada, PA-5997.

The arrival at Plymouth in October 1914 of the transports carrying the first contingent of the Canadian Expeditionary Force (the C.E.F.). They arrived only ten weeks after the declaration of war.
Public Archives Canada, PA-22708.

Valcartier," it was the soldiers who marched incessantly, drilled to exhaustion, and loathed Hughes, who were the real heroes of Valcartier. On October 3 these soldiers sailed from Gaspé for Europe. As Hughes bade his boys farewell, the soldiers responded appropriately by tossing litter from the security of the ship's deck at the Minister of Militia standing below.

In one sense, however, Sam Hughes and the departing soldiers agreed: both looked forward to the onset of the battle. They were not alone. Many Canadian manufacturers saw the war as a catalyst for renewed economic prosperity; the manu-

facturers' journal expressed this view in the autumn of 1914 without a trace of embarrassment. Other Canadians such as the Toronto police magistrate, soldier and Imperialist, Colonel George Denison, claimed the war would restore those martial virtues in which his contemporary Canadians were so deficient. Even a few of Borden's closest colleagues treated the war as an opportunity, not as a national tragedy. Robert Rogers, the party's chief organizer, saw the war as a repudiation of pre-war Liberal policy; Laurier's irresponsible attitude during the naval debate in 1912 and 1913 would now cost Canadian lives. From this analysis Rogers drew a predictable conclusion: Laurier must be punished by the Canadian electorate. Fortunately Borden and several other ministers feared the threat to national unity inherent in such a campaign and refused to agree to Rogers' recommendations. Besides, Laurier had already promised a party truce. For the Conservatives to call an election might appear unpatriotic to many Canadians. Accordingly, there was no election, and the failure of Rogers' proposal to "hive the Grits" proved that the old political game was to have new rules in wartime, a fact which many politicians were slow to appreciate and reluctant to accept.

The decision not to call an election may have been unfortunate. The bipartisan parliamentary support for the war and the decision not to hold an election obscured real differences in the attitudes of Canadians towards the war and misled both the politicians and the people. Although the declaration of war was greeted with enthusiastic demonstrations, intertwined flags and stirring oratory in Montreal and Quebec, the celebration was more ritual than the expression of spontaneous feeling. In reality, there was little excitement and much apprehension in French Canada in the first months of the war. The press of rural Quebec, for instance, betrayed marked suspicion of involvement in "foreign wars" and indifference to the nuances of the conflict. In the city of Montreal the milling crowds in front of recruiting offices in English areas of the city contrasted sharply with the peaceful sidewalks in front of recruiting offices in the French sector. There were certainly some French Canadians who vigorously supported the war effort but the majority of the French-Canadian population thought the war was a British war, not a conflict fought in their own national interests.

Berlin, Ontario, with many citizens of German origin, was an unhappy city after war broke out in 1914. Anti-German feeling ran high, and a statue of Kaiser Wilhelm was pulled down and thrown into the lake in Victoria Park. Here it is being retrieved from the waters. In 1916 the name of the city was changed to Kitchener. *Kitchener-Waterloo Record*

BERLIN AND ITS NAME

A FREE DISCUSSION OF THE METHODS
OF THE PROMOTERS OF THE CHANGE

THE UNTOWARD RESULTS

Berlin long enjoyed unity at home and high credit abroad. Now we are a community divided and ridiculed. This misfortune was not brought upon us from without. It sprang from within, and is due to the follies of the promoters of the change of name

THE PICKED MEETING
(February 11th, 1916)

The inaugural meeting of the movement at 3 P. M. on Feb. 11th in the City Hall, at which the City Council was asked to take steps to change the name of the city, was a picked meeting and was so planned, that the general public should not know of it, until it was past. The meeting was not advertised. The first knowledge that the general public had of it, was from the News-Record and Telegraph in the evening of the same day. All that the News-Record could give of the meeting in that issue, was a small item with a copy of the cut and dried resolution, which that paper received barely in time for press. The Telegraph, whose staff were identified with the promoters, devoted to the meeting the leading and most prominent article.

Broadside opposing the change of name from Berlin to Kitchener. *Metropolitan Toronto Library Board.*

Many new Canadians also did not share Robert Borden's conception of the nature of the war. A few of the foreign language newspapers in the Canadian West even expressed support for the German and Austro-Hungarian cause, a good indication of the isolation of many immigrant communities. Naturally, such scattered incidents of dissent began to inflame anti-German feeling. The understandable reluctance of German Canadians to take up arms against their homeland led immediately to strident demands that all "enemy aliens," four hundred thousand in total, should lose their citizenship rights and be subject to close scrutiny and restriction, perhaps even internment. When the government hesitated to act, individuals took matters into their own hands.

Berlin, a prosperous industrial city in Southwestern Ontario, had been settled first by German Mennonites from Pennsylvania and later by immigrants from the German Confederation and Wilhelmine Germany. Because persons of German ancestry made up almost three-quarters of the city's population, German language and culture flourished, though the surrounding area was overwhelmingly British in culture and ancestry. Not surprisingly, Berlin's enlistments lagged

The excitement of war in Europe united the sympathies of North Americans. John Philip Sousa led his U.S. Marine Band in a march down Toronto's University Avenue.
James Collection, City of Toronto Archives.

considerably behind nearby communities with the result that the local battalion needed outside reinforcement. Embarrassed and angered by the patent indifference shown towards the war and also by the Germanic milieu in which it was stationed, it became a vigilante group. In the first months of the war, a statue of the German Kaiser Wilhelm in the local park was pulled down and thrown into a nearby pond; when it was retrieved, it was melted down to make souvenir napkin holders. The oldest German social club in the community was raided, its piano tossed out a second storey window, its members bullied and sometimes beaten. A Lutheran pastor who dared to continue preaching to his parishioners in German (the only language many understood) was assaulted and dragged through the city's streets, a reminder to other German Canadians of their fate if they also transgressed. Berlin's manufacturers began to notice their orders were declining; they moved to change the city's name. In 1916, after a hotly contested plebiscite, Berlin became Kitchener, a name which honoured a British hero and effaced a reminder of the German past. The residents of Kitchener, however, were soon to learn that simply changing a name would not purchase patriotic respectability.

The German Canadians, the French Canadians and most other Canadians fervently hoped and, indeed, expected that the war would be brief, but this early optimism soon faded. As the enormity of Canada's task became apparent, the war became more controversial and its supporters more committed. In early 1915, reports of casualties appeared in Canadian newspapers, first in large notices on front pages, then as long lists on inside pages, while the front pages covered the great battles themselves. The gas attack at Ypres in April 1915 was the First Canadian Division's horrible initiation to war. It was in the following month, when 2,468 Canadians fell fighting for "one small orchard and two muddy ditches," as John Swettenham has described the battlefield, that a sombre and uncharacteristically reflective Robert Borden wrote in his diary: "This war is the suicide of civilization."

This appreciation of the stakes in the conflict led Borden to raise the number of troops that Canada would supply to

Posters promoting the sale of Victory Bonds varied widely in their appeal, as this and the example overleaf illustrate. *Public Archives Canada, TC-563 and TC-566.*

150,000 in the summer of 1915, 250,000 by fall, and 500,000 on New Year's Day 1916. For a nation of eight million to raise this number would require a massive effort; many said it would be impossible. Sir Thomas Shaughnessy, President of the Canadian Pacific Railway, publicly suggested that the economy could not endure such a great loss of manpower. How, Shaughnessy asked, could Canada continue to produce munitions and foodstuffs on a large scale if she lost her workers? Moreover, would not the cost of supporting an army of 500,000 bankrupt the country? Shaughnessy's concerns were largely valid: neither Borden nor his ministers appreciated the strain this large commitment would put upon the voluntary sys-

OPPOSITE
On the homefront, the war effort extended even into the kitchen, as housewives were reminded to save scraps for recycling into war materials.
Public Archives Canada, TC-933.

BONES & FAT
PROVIDE GLYCERINE FOR
MAKING EXRLOSIVES
GLUE FOR MAKING
AEROPLANES
FERTILISERS FOR
FOOD PRODUCTION

**START A BONE
& FAT BUCKET
TO-DAY**

Sell Contents to
General Dealers
or hand to Dustman

SAVE THEM FOR MUNITIONS

Cartridge cases in the storage area of a Hamilton factory. As the war progressed, munitions were manufactured in Canada on a substantial scale.
Public Archives Canada, PA-24451 and PA-24450.

tem of recruitment and upon the nation's economy. Already in 1915 Finance Minister Thomas White had been forced to employ new devices of uncertain merit to finance the war effort. There was no time for long range planning: White himself had admitted in 1914 that "it is not possible for my Department to estimate two weeks ahead with any degree of accuracy what the financial situation will be. We simply have to go along day by day." Thus, after promising that there would be no inflation, the Finance Department simply issued notes to meet its monetary requirements, an action certain to cause inflation. For the first time and with some reluctance, the Dominion government turned to the New York market to float a loan in 1915. An equally important precedent which occurred in that same year was the first domestic loan of $50,000,000. The enthusiastic purchase of these bonds by Canadians – it was doubly subscribed as were the later and larger "Victory Loan" campaigns – belied White's pessimistic view of the Canadian capital market. But these schemes were not enough. In 1917, White introduced an income tax to Canada, a measure he had always opposed. Canadian 1917 tax rates were lower than the 1917 British and American rates, but this was small consolation to White.

Despite the "ad hoc" character of wartime financial planning, White did succeed in acquiring the necessary finances to satisfy the voracious appetites of Canadian industry and the Canadian military machine. That he did so is a tribute to his own flexibility and inventiveness and to the willingness of many Canadians at home to share in a small way the sacrifices made by Canadian soldiers in France. Similarly, Borden's call for an army of 500,000 did not rest on a serious assessment of the manpower situation but rather upon a profound faith in the willingness of the Canadian people to accept their burden. His gamble, however, was much riskier than the Victory Loans. If he lost, the price could be conscription and national disunity.

To assure a positive response to this call, the middle class and urban English Canadians who shared Borden's goals formed an extraordinary number of voluntary bodies to persuade Canadians generally of the justice of the war and to serve the needs of those dislocated by the conflict. A few organizations such as the Toronto Anti-German League were, as the name suggests, openly propagandist and had no social service ideals. Others such as the Vacant Lot Garden Club served the war's needs in a subtler and supplementary form.

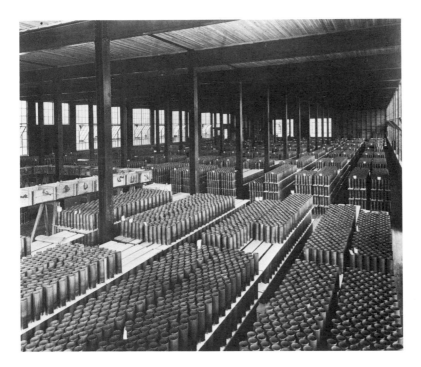

These three paintings are reproduced with the kind permission of Canadian War Museum, National Museum of Man, National Museums Canada.

INTO BATTLE. The First Canadian Division landing at St. Nazaire, France, in February 1915, bound for the Western Front.
Painting by Edgar Bundy.
Acc. No. 8121

PASSCHENDAELE. Alfred Bastien's striking painting of Canadian gunners in the mud. The battle was fought in the last days of October and the first days of November 1917.
Acc. No. 8095

FLANDERS FIELDS. *The Cambrai Road* by Maurice Cullen. The picture illustrates the way in which even a small hill could dominate a whole landscape, and helps to explain the bloody battles that were fought to gain possession of them.
Acc. No. 8143

POPULAR PRICED MIDDY
86-810. Girl's Middy of White Jean Cloth, is fashioned in slip-over style, with sailor collar, bands on three-quarter sleeve, top of pocket, and lower edge of middy of striped Jean. Colors White with trimmings of Rose, Copen or Navy stripes. Sizes 6, 8, 10, 12 and 14 years. Price **85c**

SKIRT OF SHEPHERD'S CHECK
86-81F. Pleated Skirt of Shepherd's Check Cotton, is made with shoulder straps. Colors Black and White. Sizes 6, 8, 10, 12 and 14 years. Price **65c**

MIDDY **85c**
SKIRT **65c**

86-811, White Jean Cloth Middy, slip-over style. All-round belt and large sailor collar are trimmed with white or colored bands; four-in-hand tie; buttoned cuffs on long sleeves. Colors all White, White with Navy, Red or Copen. Sizes 6 to 14 years. **85c**

JEAN SKIRT
86-81X. Separate pleated Skirt of White Jean Cloth is mounted on White Cotton underbodice, buttoned band. Sizes 6, 8, 10, 12, 14 years. **69c**

86-817. White Jean Middy, laces at the neck, patch pockets. Large sailor collar, elbow sleeves. Color all White. Sizes 6 to 14 years. Price.. **63c**

86-81B. Corduroy Velveteen Skirt, fastens under overlapping front seam, patch pockets. Colors Brown or Navy. Sizes 6 to 14 years. **1.50**

86-81A. New middy in slip-over style with collar. Closing is with tie drawn through by the fulness is caught fancy stitching. A three-quarter sleeve. White, White with trim. Sizes 6 to 14 Price

86-812. Pleated Cotton Serge, has of self mate at the back strap of Blac 6 to 14 year 19, 22, 25 28 inches. P

WOMEN'S BATHING SUIT
86-814. Cotton Jersey Cloth fashions this becoming Bathing Suit, made in two pieces. Skirt fastens on to pearl buttons at the waistband, so may be easily discarded. White bands finish V-shaped neck, front of waist and skirt and short sleeves. Attached bloomers are finished with elastic at the knees. These suits are often chosen by women for gymnasium wear. Colors Navy with White trimmings. Sizes 32, 34, 36, 38, 40. Price **1.75**

1.75

59¢

JEAN MIDDY
86-818. Jaunty Middy of White Jean Cloth is made in slip-over style and laces at the neck. Sailor collar and buttoned cuffs on long sleeves are of white or colored Jean, trimmed with rows of white braid. Pipings on pocket and lower edge of middy match collar. Colors all White, White with Red, White with Cadet. Sizes 6, 8, 10, 12 and 14 years. Price **79c**

86-819. Pleated Skirt of All-wool Serge has band and shoulder straps of Black Sateen. Sizes 6, 8, 10, 12, 13 and 14 years. Price. **1.75**

2.95

SMART, ATTRACTIVE BATHING SUIT
86-815. Very smart Woman's Bathing Suit of Aquatic Cotton suiting, made in a laced and belted style, reminding one of the popular middy. Colored Silk is utilized for the large sailor collar, bands on short sleeves and finish on lower edge of skirt and the matching laces carry out the effective color scheme. Roomy bloomers, attached beneath the belt, have elastic at the knee. This suit will be a favorite choice of the woman who is particular about her appearance both in and out of the water, and also for the gymnasium. Colors Black with Cerise or White, Navy with Paddy Green, American Beauty or White. Sizes 34 to 44 bust. Price **2.95**

GIRL'S BATHING SUIT
86-813. Serviceable Bathing Suit for girl or child, is made of Cotton Jersey Cloth, in a sleeveless style which buttons on the left shoulder. Waist and loose knee bloomers come in one piece, and the skirt is securely attached to form a long-waisted effect. Color Navy only. Sizes 4, 6, 8, 10, 12, 14 years. Price. **59c**

86-816. Girl's Slip-over White Jean, has sailor pocket trimmed with wi bands. Tie passes throug neck. Elbow sleeves fini Colors all White, White Navy. Sizes 6, 8, 10,

86-81D. Kilted Skirt Black or Red and Blac Waistband and shoulder Sizes 6, 8, 10, 12, 14 Price

By 1917 it was surely the exceptional man or woman among middle-class English Canadians who was not involved in one of these groups. Professionals and community leaders were, in fact, likely to be involved in several.

Because the military's demand for men was so great and because men at home were preoccupied with business, agriculture or other vocational pursuits, much of the volunteer work fell upon Canadian women. Emerging from the home, Canadian women took up their new tasks with great alacrity. Although men made up the executive of nearly all branches of the ubiquitous Canadian Patriotic Fund, essentially a social service agency supported by voluntary contributions, women undertook most of the work of tending for those left at home when the soldiers went off to Europe and caring for those same soldiers when they returned, often destitute and handicapped. The sight of the returned, wounded soldier, or the news of the death of a friend, a brother or a son, led to redoubled efforts and sometimes to stridency and hysteria. Those who served or whose husbands or brothers served demanded that others accept their share of the burden: a society in wartime could not tolerate human drones. With the zeal of crusaders, patriotic groups challenged the "slackers" on street corners, in churches, and in private homes, shaming them with charges of cowardice and treason.*

The intensity of the domestic war effort altered many English Canadians' view of their society. Women serving the nation in the homes, in voluntary groups, and, increasingly, in fields and factories, began to ask why men who shirked their duty should possess civil rights which they were denied. This does not mean that Canadian women became radicals who rejected the family and the home. For example, Nellie McClung, a schoolteacher and an eloquent spokesman for women's suffrage, believed that the war had given new substance to traditional arguments. In her 1915 book, *In Times Like These*, she argued that the war, the complacency, and the corruption were proof of the iniquity of rule by one-half of the world — "and not the more spiritual half." Women would not be sullied by participation in the Canadian political system; on the contrary, the system itself would be purified

OPPOSITE
The middy blouse, the height of style in 1917, adorns little girls on the pages of Eaton's Spring and Summer catalogue. *Archives, Eaton's of Canada Limited.*

---

*A young Methodist complained to the *Christian Guardian*, the Methodist paper, "I cannot go to a public meeting, I cannot walk down the street, I cannot even go home and read *Youth and Service* or *The Guardian* without being told I am a shirker." His pleas fell upon deaf ears: he was told to enlist.

*These three paintings are reproduced with
the kind permission of Canadian War
Museum, National Museum of Man,
National Museums Canada.*

ABOVE
ON LEAVE, by Clare
Atwood. The sign in
English suggests that the
scene was in England —
probably in a canteen
adjacent to a railway
station, where the men,
tired but relaxed, could
get coffee and a sandwich
after crossing from France.
Acc. No. 8019

ABOVE OPPOSITE
WAR RECORD, by
Stanley Turner. A glimpse
of the human cost of war.
Acc. No. 8907.

BELOW OPPOSITE
VICTORY. *The Return
to Mons,* by Inglis
Sheldon-Williams. The
7th Canadian Brigade
entered the town on
November 11, 1918, and
when it had been cleared
of Germans, the pipes of
the 42nd Battalion played
through the streets.
Acc. No. 8969

through the infusion of the higher principles of womankind. If rule by men meant war by men, rule with women would bring peace. The arguments of women like Mrs. McClung became more difficult to counter, and politicians learned the perils of resisting them. The defeat of Manitoba's Conservative Premier Rodmond Roblin, who had airily dismissed the plea for female suffrage, owed much to the campaign of Nellie McClung and her legion of followers. The new Manitoba Premier, T. C. Norris, rewarded the women by granting them the franchise, the first Canadian premier to do so. Within six years, women in every province except Quebec could vote, and even in Quebec women could cast a ballot in federal elections.

The success of the drive for the women's vote was a symbol and an incentive for advocates of other social goals. The nature of the war broke down limits on the conception of what Canadian society could achieve and, perhaps more important, what it should achieve. The war had brought enormous burdens, but it had also brought great opportunities, "the greatest of the ages," an exuberant Sir Clifford Sifton

Air Training Plan, First World War style. An instructor explaining the functioning of the famous JN-4 biplane, the standard trainer of the day.
Public Archives Canada, C-20396.

Ralph Connor (Rev. Charles W. Gordon), whose widely read novels reflected aspects of social conditions in Canada. He is shown in his uniform as wartime chaplain of the 43rd Cameron Highlanders of Canada.
Public Archives Canada, C-19115.

declared in 1917. Canadian soldiers in Europe were giving up their lives in a struggle for "civilization"; Canadians at home could and must use the war to make their own society a purer and better one. The war called forth exceptional selflessness, dedication, honour and sobriety. These qualities, reformers declared, must not be lost when peace returned. From the pulpits and the recruiting platforms, speakers combined appeals for a greater war effort with predictions of a national moral regeneration. Often the descriptions of the "new world" were cloaked in obscurity, but the demands were surprisingly direct and were marked by a common theme: individual sacrifice was the foundation of the common good.

ALLAN LINE

H.M.S. ALSATIAN, FLAG SHIP MERCANTILE CRUISER SQUADRON

St. Lawrence Sailings Season 1915

Montreal - Quebec to Liverpool
(ROYAL MAIL SERVICE)

From LIVERPOOL	STEAMERS	From MONTREAL		From LIVERPOOL	STEAMERS	From MONTREAL
Fri. April 30	GRAMPIAN	Fri. May 14		Fri. Aug. 6	HESPERIAN	Fri. Aug. 20
Fri. May 14	HESPERIAN	Fri. " 28		Fri. " 20	GRAMPIAN	Fri. Sep. 3
Fri. " 28	GRAMPIAN	Fri. June 11		Fri. Sep. 3	HESPERIAN	Fri. " 17
Fri. June 11	HESPERIAN	Fri. " 25		Fri. " 17	GRAMPIAN	Fri. Oct. 1
Fri. " 25	GRAMPIAN	Fri. July 9		Fri. Oct. 1	HESPERIAN	Fri. " 15
Fri. July 9	HESPERIAN	Fri. " 23		Fri. " 15	GRAMPIAN	Fri. " 29
Fri. " 23	GRAMPIAN	Fri. Aug. 6		Fri. " 29	HESPERIAN	Fri. Nov. 12

Montreal - Quebec to Glasgow

From GLASGOW	STEAMERS	From MONTREAL		From GLASGOW	STEAMERS	From MONTREAL
Sat. April 24	PRETORIAN	Sat. May 8		Sat. Aug. 14	CORSICAN	Sat. Aug. 28
Sat. May 8	SCANDINAVIAN	Sat. " 22		Sat. " 28	SCANDINAVIAN	Sat. Sep. 11
Sat. " 22	CORSICAN	Sat. June 5		Sat. Sep. 11	CORSICAN	Sat. " 25
Sat. June 5	SCANDINAVIAN	Sat. " 19		Sat. " 25	SCANDINAVIAN	Sat. Oct. 9
Sat. " 19	CORSICAN	Sat. July 3		Sat. Oct. 9	CORSICAN	Sat. " 23
Sat. July 3	SCANDINAVIAN	Sat. " 17		Sat. " 23	SCANDINAVIAN	Sat. Nov. 6
Sat. " 17	CORSICAN	Sat. " 31		Sat. Nov. 6	CORSICAN	Sat. " 20
Sat. " 31	SCANDINAVIAN	Sat. Aug. 14				

Sailings from St. John, N.B. and Halifax, N.S. to Liverpool

From ST. JOHN	STEAMERS	From HALIFAX		From ST. JOHN	STEAMERS	From HALIFAX
Wed. Mar. 24	HESPERIAN	Thu. Mar .25		Wed. Apr. 21	CORSICAN	Thu. Apr. 22
Fri. April 2	SCANDINAVIAN	Sat. April 3		Fri. " 30	HESPERIAN	Sat. May 1

Tickets for Sale Here

Until the sinking of the *Lusitania*, in May 1915, made it clear that Germany intended to sink passenger liners without warning, Atlantic sailing schedules were widely advertised. The Allan liner *Hesperian*, included in this 1915 schedule, was soon to be a victim. Her sailing from Liverpool on September 3 was her last; she was torpedoed the next day by U-20, the same U-boat that sank the *Lusitania*.
Corporate Archives, Canadian Pacific.

Sir Thomas Shaughnessy, President of the Canadian Pacific Railway. In 1916 when Borden announced intentions to supply an army of 500 000 for European combat, Shaughnessy expressed fears that the loss of so many workers would bankrupt the nation. *Public Archives Canada, C-6650.*

One of the first personal indulgences offered for sacrifice upon the altar of war was alcohol. To the time-honoured arguments for outlawing John Barleycorn, a new and powerful one was added: patriotism. Industrial inefficiency, broken homes and ravaged bodies were the social costs of alcohol use, and in wartime such costs were criminal. Since an 1898 liquor plebiscite which had shown a slight majority for prohibition in Canada as a whole and a fairly large majority for prohibition in English Canada, anti-alcohol sentiment had grown and consumption had decreased. Drink's supporters were mainly in Quebec and among new Canadians and the labouring classes, all segments of the Canadian population which the largely British middle-class patriotic groups had come to regard with an increasing degree of suspicion during the war. So completely did prohibitionist forces rout their opposition that by 1916 every province in the Dominion had enacted prohibition legislation, with one significant and rather ominous exception — Quebec. But very soon even Quebec succumbed to the national tide, an event which the Montrealer, Stephen Leacock, greeted with melancholy:

> Very dreadful, not a doubt. Alcohol is doomed; it is going; it is gone. Yet when I think of a hot Scotch on a winter evening, or a gin rickey beside a tennis court, or a stein of beer on a bench beside a bowling green, . . . I wish somehow we could prohibit the use of alcohol and merely drink beer and whiskey and gin as we used to.

Of course, the prohibitionists did not share these regrets as they fervently proclaimed that Canada had become a land fit for heroes and a land whose heroes would remain morally and physically fit.

Probably the most effective, and certainly the most strident, advocates of prohibition and other measures of "moral reform" were the Protestant churches of English Canada. Prior to the war, these churches, especially the Methodists and the Presbyterians, had become most critical of the indifference to poverty, the selfishness, and the inequality of Canadian society and had begun to talk of the need for a national regeneration. In 1906, for example, the General Conference of the Methodist Church had declared that its work was to "set up the Kingdom of God among men, . . . a social order founded on the principles of the Gospel." The war seemed to offer a golden opportunity for such a reconstruction of society. Protestant leaders became Christian soldiers who identified the Canadian role in the war with the Church's struggle against evil. At Toronto's wealthy Timothy Eaton Memorial Church, the Methodist, James Henderson, comforted mothers who had lost their sons by telling them that their sons had "accomplished far more for Canada, for the Empire, for the world, for Christ, done more to bring about a new order of things in a few months than you or I could ever do if we lived a thousand years." In short, Canada's participation in the war against the infidel would create "a new order of things" in which social justice, faith and service would be pre-eminent values. The triumph of prohibition seemed a confirmation of this interpretation of the war, and it heightened the demands both for further reform and for enlistment. In the years between 1914 and 1918, one sees the best and worst characteristics of Canadian Protestantism; on the one hand, its idealism and energy and, on the other hand, its excessive

Northern River, by Tom Thomson,
perhaps his most famous picture, painted
in 1915. He was drowned two years
later, but he had profoundly influenced
the painters who formed the famous
Group of Seven in 1919, just as Borden's
years of leadership were ending.
The National Gallery of Canada, Ottawa.

righteousness and shallow, sometimes racist, nationalism.

This surge of nationalism in English Canada was one of the most remarkable developments of the First World War. Like most nationalisms, wartime English-Canadian nationalism blended an often mystical view of the past with a brilliant vision of the nation's future. Canada was making its own mark in the world, and a distinguished one it was. There was a pride of accomplishment and a sense of maturity which Canadians had earlier lacked that wartime songs, poems, newspapers and public oratory all reflected. *The Major*, a 1917 novel by the best-selling novelist, Ralph Connor, expressed in a dramatic, if rather trite, form the belief that the nation's accomplishments mirrored the individual growth of her citizens. When Larry, a Canadian who had been working in Chicago, met his former classmate and future wife, Jane, he

> could hardly believe his eyes and ears, so immense was the change that had taken place in Jane during these ten months [of war]. He could hardly believe, . . . that this brilliant, quick-witted radiant girl was the quiet, demure Jane of his college days. . . .

What, Larry asked,

> had released those powers of mind and soul which he could now recognise as being her own, but which he had never seen in action? As in a flash it came to him that the mighty change was due to the terrible energising touch of war.

Almost unnoticed because of the war, an important Canadian Arctic Expedition, led by Vilhjalmur Stefansson, spent fruitful years in the far north. Stefansson devoted himself to exploration and filled in the last important gaps in the map of the Canadian Arctic. R. M. Anderson, second in command, directed the scientific studies. This snapshot of Anderson was taken south of Cape Krusenstern in February 1916.
Public Archives Canada, C-30864.

Internment camps quickly became a necessity in wartime. This one in Vernon, B.C. housed its inmates in specially built huts. Others used commandeered buildings. *Public Archives Canada, C-17583.*

The nation and the individual had become one in purpose and achievement.

Even if Canadian literature, as exemplified by *The Major*, had not itself achieved a new maturity, Connor's phrases reflected the ideal of the new nationalism. *The New Era in Canada*, a selection of patriotic essays published in 1917, revealed another strain in English-Canadian nationalism, the exaltation of the state and its power for good. Its preface boldly declared that "the test of national greatness lies in willing service to the state." War had created the "national superstructure" which would endure and create new opportunities for service in peacetime. In this light, citizenship became not merely a matter of birthplace but primarily a question of service. The "new era" would be distinguished by a stronger, more centralized government which expressed the nation's will and which, paternalistically, drew out the best from the citizens. But who would decide where the "national interest" lay? To be sure, Ralph Connor had no doubt, nor did many other English Canadians in 1916 or 1917. There were many others, however, who neither shared their outlook nor grasped at "the opportunity" for service. And it was this difference among Canadians in the perception of the war which troubled politicians — including Robert Borden.

Borden, an English Canadian of moderate Imperialist and progressive beliefs, shared the view that the war represented the overwhelming national interest. Moreover, Borden generally accepted the aims of the social reformers of English Canada, particularly their desire to strengthen the apparatus of government. He had long deplored the rudimentary character of government, the use of patronage as a system of recruitment for the civil service, and the corruption endemic in the pre-war party system. But in Ottawa, if not in Toronto, one could sense that not all Canadians shared this view of the national interest. In Borden's own party, a man like Bob Rogers, a sworn foe of prohibition and of the reformist Norris Liberal government in Manitoba, despised reform politicians and almost all they stood for. Politics, Rogers would say, are a man's game and are not a pursuit for whimpering clerics and women. Even more disturbing to the Prime Minister was the abundant evidence that the "Win the War" movement in English Canada possessed hysterical and perhaps even violent impulses. Thus, when the Rev. Charles Gordon (Ralph Connor) denounced Canada's "drones" and called for compulsory service, Borden regarded the effort as foolish and harmful. And Borden's fears had a strong basis: the growing indifference and, in some cases, antipathy to the war which was being

The celebration of Christmas Day 1916 in one of the internment camps. *Public Archives Canada, C-14104.*

expressed in French Canada.

The war had bred not one nationalism but two. To the taunts of disloyalty from their English-Canadian countrymen, French Canadians responded with anger and bitterness. They pointed to the government's disgraceful treatment of French Canadians in the early days of the war, the appointment of a Methodist Minister to recruit in French Catholic Quebec, and Sam Hughes the Orangeman, and his dubious leadership of the Canadian war effort. The major grievance of French Canada, however, was the Conservative government in Ontario and its apparent desire to end French instruction in Ontario schools. This issue transcended Ontario's boundaries in 1916 when Ernest Lapointe, a young Liberal Member of Parliament, introduced a resolution in the House of Commons calling for the restoration of the use of French in Ontario schools. In fact, even if the resolution had passed, there was very little that the federal government could have done; education was clearly a provincial responsibility. But this was ignored in the uproar that followed. Lapointe and Laurier bluntly asked how they could persuade French Canadians to fight for a nation which did not respect the fundamental right of French Cana-

THE NEWEST CORSET AND UNDERWEAR

LIGHT-WEIGHT

19-1916
39¢

19-301 VEST
39¢

19-9175
2.00

FLEECE-LINED

19-302 DRAWERS
39¢

THE NEW COLLIER-CUT COMBINATION, IN LIGHT WEIGHT, AT THE EXTREMELY LOW PRICE OF 39c

19-1916. Although low-priced it embraces all the special features of the higher-priced Collier-cut garments. Priced so low as to be within reach of all. This new style of combination will be welcomed by many women. Made so when being worn, it is **always closed**, although it is called open crotch. It eliminates the unpleasant features of the regular open crotch combination. Made of very fine ribbed cotton, light weight, in the spring needle stitch; low neck; yoke neatly trimmed, elbow length sleeves, ankle length. A splendid Combination, which is sure to be popular. **Sizes 32 to 40.**
Price..**.39**

THE LATEST

CORSET MODEL

MEDIUM IN EVERY RESPECT

19-9175. It is a splendid combination of fit, style and grace. Note the shorter skirt, the slightly curved waist, and the higher bust, with special gores to give absolute comfort. This corset is a beauty, made of brocade with fancy silk pattern, and is lined with good quality of cotton to give it extra strength. Silk embroidery trimmed bust, with draw-string. Of course it would usually sell for considerably more, and, at this low price, the quantity we have should not last long; so order early and secure perfect corset comfort. Suitable for medium figures. **Sizes 19 to 24.** Price...........**2.00**

NEW STYLE OF WEAVE IN THIS WOMAN'S "YORKNIT" FLEECE-LINED VEST, AT A SPECIAL PRICE

19-301. This Woman's Fleece-Lined Vest is made by an entirely new process, and represents wonderful value. Vest lined throughout with a nice, soft, heavy, even fleece and is particularly nice for women who cannot stand the touch of wool. High neck, long sleeves, buttoned front. The opportunity this presents does not come often, so take advantage of the low price. **White only. Sizes 32 to 38.**
Price...**.39**

19C-302. **Closed, Ankle-Length Drawers** to match.
Price...**.39**

19D-302. **Open Ankle-Length Drawers** to match.
Price...**.39**

An officer and his bride.
Public Archives Canada,
PA-8179.

dians to use their language. *Le Droit*, an Ottawa newspaper, was more candid: "Of what use is it for us to fight against Prussianism and barbarity [in Europe] when the same conditions exist at home?" Many English Canadians had a prompt answer: "When French Canadians show themselves willing to preserve the nation by enlisting in satisfactory numbers, then they may have special privileges, but not before."

When the vote on Lapointe's resolution was finally taken, many English-Canadian Liberals deserted Sir Wilfrid Laurier and opposed the resolution. In the province of Ontario itself, the Liberal Opposition Leader, Newton Rowell, supported the government's language policy. Most adamant, perhaps, were the Western Canadian Liberals. The prominent Manitoba Liberal, J. W. Dafoe, charged that Lapointe's resolution was sufficient proof that the traitor, Henri Bourassa, controlled the minds of Liberal Party leaders. There could be no compromise. To Dafoe, the aged Laurier had lost his grasp of the helm and sinister forces had seized the command. To Laurier, English-Canadian Liberals were undermining the party when its opportunity was greatest and were pandering to the racist and the demagogue. There could be neither compromise nor understanding.

Robert Borden derived only small satisfaction from the Liberals' troubles. Behind them lurked a tension which threatened Confederation, and, as a Prime Minister and a politician, Borden naturally feared increasing that tension. But by 1917 Borden had little sympathy for French Canada's complaints. "The vision of the French Canadian is very limited," Borden wrote in January 1917. "He is not well informed and he is in a condition of extreme exasperation by reason of fancied wrongs supposed to be inflicted upon his compatriots in other provinces, especially Ontario." The impact of war had broken down not only those tender threads which bound together French and English Canada, but also the normal restraints upon national political leaders. By the third year of the war, Canada had truly become, in the novelist Hugh Maclennan's eloquent phrase, "a nation of two solitudes."

5

The Clash

BEFORE DAWN on Easter morning 1917 Canadian soldiers moved towards the German lines. At 5:30 a.m. an incredible din signalled the start of the attack; wave after wave of Canadian troops swamped the German defences until by the end of the day the Germans were in retreat, the field of battle was littered with dead, and bloody water filled the shell holes. The Canadians completed their task with awesome efficiency: Vimy Ridge, a symbol of the German war machine's early ascendancy, had fallen to the once despised colonial forces. Easter 1917 was the Canadian Corps' finest hour.

At home, the triumph at Vimy heightened patriotic zeal among the mothers, brothers and friends who anxiously followed the progress of the Canadian Expeditionary Force. For many, pride mingled with sorrow; 3,600 Canadian lives were lost in the brief moment of battle at Vimy. Even worse, Vimy was not the end but only a beginning of the bloodiest, darkest and most eventful year of the war. Nineteen seventeen had begun with rumours of peace, as the German army weakened and the German people suffered because of the food blockade carried out by Allied ships. But in March there was bad news. The intensified German submarine attacks on allied shipping threatened to cut the lifeline between Britain and her New World arsenal. Even worse, the Czar of Russia abdicated in the wake of revolution, and the Eastern Front seemed sure to collapse. There was some consolation in April: Woodrow Wilson, whose autumn 1916 campaign slogan, "He kept us out of war" had angered many Canadians, led "the great peaceful people" of the United States into "the most terrible and disastrous of all wars." But was there time for the Americans to set foot upon French soil before the final battle began? No answer was available in the spring of 1917.

Borden was in an excellent position to determine the seriousness of the military situation. At the request of Britain's Prime Minister, David Lloyd George, he had gone to London in February to attend sessions of the Imperial War Cabinet and the Imperial War Conference. Here, Borden and the other Dominion Prime Ministers met with the Prime Minister of Britain and with the inner cabinet directing the war. For the first time, the Dominions were permitted a voice in Imperial war policy and were given the information necessary to make the voice a responsible one. Not surprisingly, Borden basked in his new Imperial role and, in London, he shared the praise lavished upon the Canadian soldiers for the victory at Vimy. But the exhilaration was tempered by the information passed

A Canadian Battalion going over the top, October, 1916. *Public Archives Canada, PA-648.*

on in the private meetings. Lloyd George warned Borden that no victory could be expected in 1917 and that hard fighting lay ahead for the Canadians. The entry of the Americans surely meant that Germany would "stake everything on the summer's operation." The supreme test, perhaps even the Allies' Armageddon, would come in 1917 before the Americans could possibly arrive.

With this knowledge, Borden asked his Minister of Militia, Edward Kemp, what the state of the Canadian Expeditionary Force was. The reply was prompt, concise and pessimistic: the voluntary system was not working; neither publicity nor patriotism could spur young men to enlist. The battle for Vimy had cost over 10,000 men, dead or wounded, but enlistment for the month of March 1917 had been only 7,300. Hearing this, Borden knew what he must do to preserve Canada's honour and to assure Allied victory. On May 18, 1917, four days after his return from Europe, he announced his intention of introducing compulsory military service to Canada. Never before had the state compelled young men to fight in a war beyond Canada's shores, and the results of Borden's decision could not be predicted. One thing was certain: there would be opposition and probably a political crisis.

Trench warfare will ever be associated with the First World War. This typical scene suggests some of the dangers and discomforts involved.
Public Archives Canada, PA-556.

In Canada's sister dominion, Australia, conscription had been twice rejected in a plebiscite. In Canada, opposition seemed even more intense, especially in French Canada. For French-Canadian Conservatives, support for conscription was tantamount to political suicide. Already on June 5, the Conservatives' strongest French-Canadian Minister, E. L. Patenaude, had resigned, denouncing conscription as a profound threat to national unity and pointing to Borden's 1914 and 1915 promises of no conscription. There were others who had misgivings about conscription. Bob Rogers, for example, sat dumbfounded on the government benches as Borden announced conscription, a policy which Rogers believed would destroy the Conservative Party in Quebec and in the immigrant areas of the Canadian West. Borden knew that Rogers' fears were largely justified but, unlike Rogers, Borden considered that the national interest took precedence over political considerations. Moreover, in the political disturbance which followed the conscription announcement, Borden perceived the dim outline of a new and more attractive political landscape.

This future prospect arose from the widespread endorsement of conscription by English-Canadian Liberals. The day after Borden's House of Commons speech, the Toronto *Globe*, the traditional mouthpiece of Ontario Liberalism, supported conscription and recommended that all Liberals should rally to Borden's call. Throughout English Canada, Liberals and Conservatives organized public meetings which issued bi-

Mud and barbed wire entanglements — two obstacles faced by the infantry in almost every major assault on the Western Front. *Newfoundland Archives.*

Casualties, October, 1916. By this point in the war, voluntary enlistments were slowing and soon Borden would be forced to face the bitter question of compulsion.
Public Archives Canada, PA-940.

partisan declarations for conscription. These events pleased Borden greatly and seemed to offer the opportunity to strengthen the war effort and to refashion the political system simultaneously. On May 25 Borden therefore proposed to his old antagonist, Sir Wilfrid Laurier, that they form a coalition to carry Canada through the national emergency, a coalition which would renounce the partisanship and patronage that had marred pre-war politics. Not since Confederation had a coalition governed Canada, but the national emergency surely justified exceptional means. To Borden and to all supporters of conscription, Liberal and Conservative, the arguments for coalition seemed irrefutable. To Laurier, however, they were specious, and on June 6, he told Borden that he could support neither coalition nor conscription.

Laurier's action was generally acclaimed by French Canadians and denounced by English Canadians. Some of Laurier's oldest English-Canadian colleagues refused to believe the reports of the Liberal leader's stand and insisted that, as in the past, Laurier would strike a compromise. But this time no compromise could be found. When the vote on the second reading of the Military Service Bill took place in early July, the depth of the national division on conscription became abundantly clear. Fifty-five Members of Parliament opposed the bill; forty-six of them were from Quebec. Only four Members from west of the Ottawa River opposed the bill as party loyalty crumbled. The considerations which caused so many English-Canadian Liberals to abandon their venerable leader are clearly suggested in the anguished reaction to the announcement of conscription by the highly partisan New Brunswick Liberal, Frank Carvell:

> There is something within me which abhors the idea of throwing up my hands when others are fighting my battles. . . . I do not know where I am going to land. I am going home this afternoon to consult with my constituents and, I may as well tell you frankly, especially my family, because after all there comes a time in the life of every man when he and his own must do some hard thinking for themselves.

Not surprisingly, Carvell and "his own" landed on the side of the conscriptionists.

Carvell's decision and that of many other Liberals heartened Borden. He could not have been encouraged, however, by the adamant French-Canadian opposition to conscription. Borden preferred a wide coalition which would encompass all groups in Canadian national life; he was even willing to delay

Soldiers load artillery during the battle of Vimy Ridge.
Public Archives Canada, PA-1083.

conscription and give up his own position to achieve this end. After Laurier's refusal, Borden had little choice but to accept a lesser goal. He could work out an accommodation with those Liberal dissenters like Carvell who, for political and personal reasons, supported his policy of conscription. There was even the hope that from such an accommodation a more progressive political party would emerge, but for the moment what mattered was victory for conscriptionist forces in the forthcoming election.

Laurier's actions nevertheless created great obstacles to the fulfillment of even this more limited aim. The delay and debate gave time for opposition to conscription to crystallize and, unfortunately, for tempers to rise. By July it was clear that any coalition government committed to conscription would not possess any meaningful French-Canadian representation. Nearly all of French Canada, even the Nationalists and the Conservatives, were uniting behind Laurier's stand against conscription. More surprising and probably more distressing to Borden was the evidence that strong resistance to conscription was present in English Canada. Most of English Canada's leaders supported conscription, of this Borden was certain; but the support of the followers was not assured. Many farm leaders, angered by untended harvests created by the war's voracious appetite for manpower, spoke out against conscription. Was not the production of food more valuable to the Empire than the presence of a few thousand more Canadians among the millions fighting in France? The argument outraged conscriptionists, but it was nonetheless difficult to counter. The rural opposition together with French-Canadian resistance made Borden's task more complex than he had first imagined and the debate angrier than he had expected.

During the summer of 1917 Canadians became more aware of national politics; never before had there been such a feeling that the national government could so profoundly affect the destiny of individual Canadians. On street corners, in churches, in town halls, Canadians raised their voices and sometimes even their fists in defence of their point of view on the conscription issue. From English Canada came demands that reinforcements for the Canadian Expeditionary Force be secured through compulsion and that French Canada be made to submit. In late 1916 Dr. Chown, the General Superintendent of the Methodist Church, had provided the text for the debate with a rhetorical question: "Is it fair to leave the province of Quebec to retain its strength in numbers, ready for any

OPPOSITE
An air view of the maze of trenches that the Allies and the Germans had dug on Vimy Ridge.
Public Archives Canada, PA-2259.

political or military aggression in the future, while our Protestants go forth to slaughter and decimation?" For Henri Bourassa, for Laurier, and for most French Canadians, the question was too outrageous to consider. They quickly responded, however, by pointing out that English Canadians had not exactly battered down the recruiting office doors. At the beginning of 1916 official statistics had shown that over sixty per cent of the enlistments were British-born and, in some rural areas of English Canada, scarcely a son was fighting in France. Since French Canada lacked British immigrants and was largely rural in character, was it really doing much less than English Canada? Exaggerated and inflammatory, such charges were the fodder for an increasingly bitter national debate.

As Prime Minister, Borden was most exposed to these tensions. Committed to conscription and coalition but realizing the potential dangers to the nation, Borden moved deliberately, keeping his own counsel. He had to form a cabinet which would embrace as many interests as possible. The goal, however, was clearer than the means. In July and August, Borden was consistently disappointed. His ally, Sir Clifford Sifton, the owner of the powerful *Manitoba Free Press* and the brother of Alberta's Liberal Premier Arthur Sifton, found that neither journalistic power nor blood relationship could bring prominent Western Canadian Liberals to Borden's side. They would support conscription, privately if not publicly, but coalition seemed out of the question. Nevertheless, a Winnipeg Liberal convention in August, which had been planned earlier to consider the future of the Liberal Party on the Prairies, offered the opportunity for Sifton to pressure Western Liberals into open support of conscription and coalition. But Sifton's attempt to direct the convention produced dissent initially and then, in unison, a refusal to follow his direction. Finally and unexpectedly, the convention declared its support for Wilfrid Laurier. The Western Liberals, it was widely rumoured, were afraid to accept conscription and coalition lest they alienate the sizeable non-Anglo-Saxon population in the West, a great number of whom had been brought to Canadian shores by Clifford Sifton. This irony was not lost upon Borden, who began to consider in more detail means of eliminating the aliens' opposition to conscription.

The weapon chosen was a blunt one: removal of the franchise. In early September, the War-time Elections Act dramatically shifted the political balance in Western Canada.

When Arthur Meighen, Borden's most articulate and candid minister, described how Canadian citizens of enemy alien birth naturalized after 1902 would lose their vote, Western Liberals despaired and fumed. The arrogance and directness of the government's move astonished the Liberals and probably a few Tories as well. Indeed, modern observers are still puzzled by this act through which Canada, alone among Allied nations, disfranchised a large part of its electorate. The explanation, however, is probably straightforward. Borden, his government, and the majority of English Canadians had decided that the needs of the war had primacy over the claims of democracy. The war would preserve and further the growth of democracy in the world; hence short term limitations on democracy were justified. The War-time Elections Act was yet another variation on an old theme: the end justifies the means.

A remarkable photograph taken on April 9, 1917, during the Battle of Vimy Ridge. A party of Germans, overrun by the initial Canadian assault, are surrendering to follow-up forces. *Public Archives Canada, PA-1123.*

This summerhouse under a dugout shows that the sense of whimsy was not completely lost in the tragedy of war.
Public Archives Canada, PA-4400.

OPPOSITE

Brigadier-General A. G. L. McNaughton, commander of the 11th Brigade C.F.A. and the Canadian Corps Heavy Artillery.
Public Archives Canada, C-23062.

If Borden had chosen to go to the country immediately on a conscriptionist platform, he almost certainly could have had his victory. The Conservatives, despondent throughout the long summer, became suddenly enthusiastic after the passing of the War-time Elections Act and another franchise bill, the Military Voter's Act which made special and, from the Tory point of view, favourable provision for the soldier's vote. But for Borden such a victory would not be satisfactory; he continued to work for a coalition government. He was soon to find that the franchise bills were his greatest asset in attaining this goal. English-Canadian Liberals, especially those from Western Canada, were quite willing to reconsider his earlier offers. Now, however, many of his own colleagues, sensing their improved position, had doubts. Yet Borden persisted and he gave his reason in his diary. "I am beginning to feel," Borden wrote in late September, "that we should take [the Liberals] in as our first duty is to win, at any cost, the coming election in order that we may continue to do our part in winning the war and that Canada not be disgraced." To the Liberals' enduring advantage, Borden placed the national interest as he perceived it above the interest of the Conservative Party.

The famous Dumbells concert party organized in 1916 by Major Merton Plunket, a Y.M.C.A. entertainment officer. It brought some lighter moments to the life of front-line troops until after the Armistice. Its two best known members were Al Plunket (second from left), the singer, and Ross Hamilton (centre), famous as a female impersonator. The company toured Canada for several seasons after the war.
Public Archives Canada, PA-5734.

Borden's decision and the Liberals' reassessment restored the possibility of coalition. Protracted negotiations with Western Canadian Liberals in early September had broken down, and on September 20, with Parliament prorogued, an exhausted Borden escaped to the Laurentians. He did not rest long. On the afternoon following his departure, a note arrived from J. D. Reid stating that Western Liberals wanted to reopen negotiations. Rcid, angered by the Westerners' indecision and confident of electoral victory without Western Liberal representation, recommended that Borden reject the Westerners. But Borden would have none of it. The negotiations began once more and on October 12 a new cabinet was announced.

By any standard the new coalition cabinet was an impressive one; most commentators called it the best in Canadian history. From Alberta came Arthur Sifton, the province's premier and, by all reports, a strong individual;* James Calder,

*Sifton tales abound. A member of one of Canada's leading Methodist families, Sifton's conduct frequently astonished, indeed scandalized, his fellow believers. On a summer Sunday morning in Edmonton, a Methodist preacher stirred his congregation to action. Did they know that within two blocks of their church stood a house of ill repute? And even on the Lord's Day its vile trade did not cease. Where the law failed, the church itself must act. Leaving their pews, the outraged parishioners marched to the brothel prepared to close it down; but there was no confrontation, only confusion. There on the brothel veranda sat the province's premier, his feet on the railing, a fat cigar in his mouth, giving all passersby a friendly nod. The Methodists dispersed quietly.

a Saskatchewan cabinet minister, brought great administrative skill and wide experience in running successful election campaigns in Western Canada. The Manitoba representative and the new Minister of Agriculture, Thomas Crerar, is particularly interesting since he had had no previous political experience and had been the president of the Grain Growers' Grain Company. Crerar gave the cabinet a non-partisan air, which was extremely important in the West where the traditional political parties were most unpopular. Crerar's presence proved to Westerners that the Union Government would not be a government like all others.

The Eastern Liberal Unionist membership in the Unionist cabinet also included two with no political experience: the Minister of Militia, S. C. Mewburn; and the Minister of Marine, Fisheries and Naval Service, C. C. Ballantyne. The others, Newton Rowell from Ontario, Frank Carvell from New Brunswick, and A. K. Maclean from Nova Scotia, were men of strong political background who promised to give major assistance in the imminent election campaign. One glaring weakness in the Unionist cabinet remained; not a single French-Canadian Liberal would join the Union Government.

The Imperial War Cabinet, May 1, 1917. In the front row are Rt. Hon. A. Henderson, Rt. Hon. Viscount Milner, Rt. Hon. The Earl Curzon of Kedleston, Rt. Hon. A. Bonar Law, Rt. Hon. David Lloyd George, Prime Minister Borden, Rt. Hon. W. F. Massey and Rt. Hon. J. C. Smuts. Sir G. H. Perley stands directly behind Borden.

Major W. A. ("Billy")
Bishop, third ranking ace
of the aerial war of
1914-18. He downed 72
enemy planes and was the
first Canadian airman to
be awarded the Victoria
Cross.
*Public Archives Canada,
PA-1654.*

OPPOSITE
Lieutenant-General Sir
Arthur Currie, who took
command of the Canadian
corps in 1917, with
General Sir Douglas Haig,
the British Commander-
in-Chief.
*Public Archives Canada,
PA-2497.*

What prompted these Liberals to accept Borden's final offer? To be sure, many, in the words of the *Grain Growers' Guide*, were men "whose love for their country [was] greater than their love for party." But patriotism was not the only motive. In the Liberal Unionists' correspondence one finds an additional motive, the desire to save the Liberal Party in English Canada. As the Liberal Unionist Fred Pardee pointed out, any government committed to conscription would sweep English Canada with or without coalition. Pardee argued that in a coalition the conscriptionist Liberals might keep their unity and later emerge to recapture the Liberal Party when the aged Laurier finally withdrew from the political stage. This scenario was not followed, but the belief in its possibility limited the loyalty of the Liberal Unionists to Unionism and understandably raised the suspicions of their Conservative colleagues.

The turmoil in Ottawa during the conscription debate mirrored similar disturbances throughout the country. The pride in the achievement of the Canadian Corps and the sorrow upon seeing ever longer lists of casualties combined to add a frantic tone to English-Canadian public gatherings. "Slackers" were harassed on the street and in their homes. In the Protestant churches, the pastors, with the vivid imagery of the King James Bible at their service, made Canada's war a struggle for Christian civilization. Satanic forces within and without the nation must be crushed; black and white, good and evil were known; there could be no compromise. As the poet Wilfred Campbell wrote:

O.2512

Canadian troops passing through the ruins of Ypres in November 1917. *Public Archives Canada, PA-40272.*

We are either on God's side or evil's
We are either perjured or true; —
And that, which we set out to do in the first place
That we must do.

But to many Canadians, especially those in Quebec, the purpose "in the first place" had been different. Rejecting the premises, these Canadians could not accept Campbell's conclusions. Thus, in the rural parishes of Quebec where the war's impact had been barely felt, the imposition of conscription was resented and feared. Young men were being asked — indeed, being compelled — to die for a cause that they could not understand. Rather than be conscripted, many of Quebec's young men, perhaps tens of thousands, fled to the remote corners of the province where the nation's law had no sway. Nearly all the rest applied for exemptions from conscription, which most eventually received. But it was not so easy for English Canadians who, for various reasons, did not want to serve. Certainly the tens of thousands of English Canadians who applied for exemptions faced an ostracism far more severe

than young French Canadians did. The military service tribunals that one faced in London, Ontario or Winnipeg showed little of the leniency of the tribunal in Quebec City.

But surely the greatest hardships befell those Canadians of German descent. Some were interned; almost all were suspected. The German language press was forced to cease publication in 1918, and the use of the German language in public places was not tolerated. Hundreds of Brauns and Schmidts became Browns and Smiths overnight and a once proud heritage was lastingly rejected. Stripped of their franchise, fearful of their neighbours, German and Austrian Canadians anxiously awaited the end of the awful conflict.

This pressure to conform is particularly significant. The diversity of Canada, which politicians, journalists and the general public now proclaim to be their nation's finest quality, was then regarded as a barrier to national greatness, an obstacle to be fought and overcome. English Canadians committed to the war effort believed that through compulsion the national state could and should create a nation more of one mind. Although the Union Government did not succeed in this task — indeed, it could not have succeeded — fascination with the possibilities for central government action continued among middle-class

The House of Commons meeting in the Victoria Memorial Museum (now the National Museum of Canada) in March 1918. This was the first session after the formation of the Union Government and the general election of December 1917. The Commons had taken refuge in the museum after the disastrous fire of 1916. *Public Archives Canada, PA-22433.*

The Prime Minister
watching a march past by
Canadian forces in France
in July 1918.
*Public Archives Canada,
PA-2746.*

English Canadians. On the other hand, the assertive national
government as represented by Unionism was feared by French
Canadians and by the so-called "enemy aliens" who saw the
central government as inimical to their way of life. For these
Canadians, the distrust of "Ottawa" was profound and enduring. Rather than creating a nation of one mind, the Union
Government had fostered fundamental divisions which con-

tinue to mark Canadian political life to this day. And it was that reality which rendered impossible Borden's dreams of a lasting Unionist party.

But in the late fall of 1917 the immediate task, the winning of the December election, permitted little time for thoughtful reflection on the future. At first, the outcome seemed certain. There was little hope of Unionist success in French Canada, but Unionists were confident that their platform would win nearly unanimous approval in the rest of Canada. Soon, doubts began to arise. Support for conscription was undoubtedly widespread in English Canada but understanding and acceptance of its consequences were not. The *Grain Growers' Guide*, for example, warned in November that unless the Unionists exempted farmers they would face "serious political consequences" in the Canadian West. In Ontario as well, the rural areas were reportedly outraged when their young men were taken from the farms while tales of extraordinary rates of exemption in Quebec circulated. Thus, in late November, a political decision was taken by Borden and Clifford Sifton: farmers, farmers' sons and agricultural workers would be exempted. The rural revolt against conscription subsided and Unionism's supremacy in English Canada was assured. But the rural revolt had ended the Unionist overconfidence, and the final days of the campaign witnessed an unparalleled emotional intensity.

Unionists assailed Laurier Liberalism as the early church did its heretics. "Make every ballot a bullet," urged the *Manitoba Free Press*, "a vote for Laurier is a vote for the Kaiser." Cartoons showed the Kaiser and Laurier celebrating a Liberal victory together. The news from the front emphasized the need for reinforcements in a horrible way. In November, a month before the election, the war's grimmest battle in the mud of Passchendaele brought death or wounds to over 15,000 Canadians. The shock at the news led the committed to redouble their electoral efforts. Maudlin appeals were made to the newly enfranchised women who were solemnly told that each vote for Union Government "will be a wreath laid on the graves of the boys who have given their lives." As the campaign progressed, it seemed almost as if the enemy came from within not from without the nation. A pungent expression of this feeling was a Canadian map printed on the front page of the *Toronto News*. All Canada was coloured imperial red except for Quebec; it was black.

On December 17, 1917, the bitterest election campaign

in Canadian history ended with a decisive Unionist victory. Borden had gathered with some intimate friends in the Senate Chamber to learn the results. A couple of days earlier the Unionists had predicted they would take 135 seats and the Liberals 97. In fact, the Unionists won 153 seats and the Liberals only 82. In a certain sense, the *Toronto News* map was accurate. Of the 82 Liberal members, no less than 62 were from Quebec. The Unionists won but three English Canadian constituencies in Quebec; the Liberals won only two seats west of the Ontario border. Could Confederation and the party system survive this division on racial lines? No one knew for certain on the morning of December 18, not even Robert Borden.

6
Peace, 1918

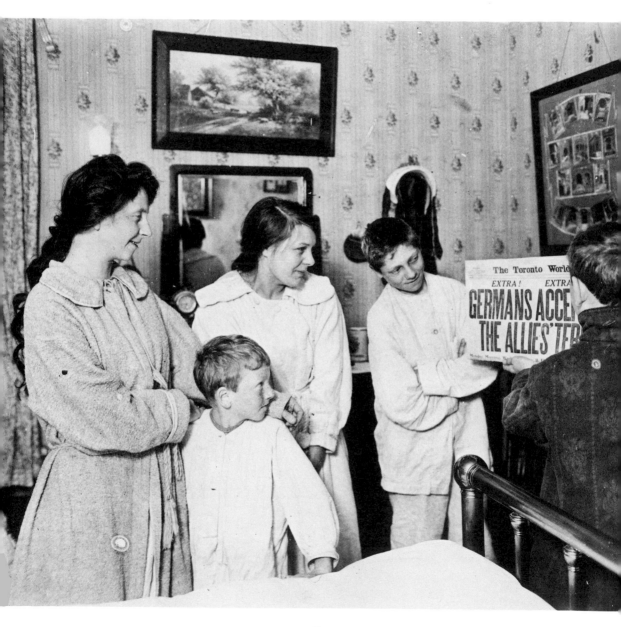

THE WAR'S END was as sudden as its beginning was protracted. In the spring of 1918, the Germans launched a ferocious attack, a last-ditch attempt to win their victory before the Americans arrived in force. Six months later, in late October, the exhausted and demoralized German Army collapsed and the Allies had their total victory. After the long journey through the deprivation, sorrow and bitterness of war, the abrupt moment of peace brought spontaneous joy in the streets of Toronto and Montreal, as it did in the streets of London and New York. For many Canadians, however, November 11 would forever remain a day of sadness, a day when they remembered one or more of the sixty thousand friends or relatives who were the Great War's victims. The memory of the dead, the "dry" parties of celebration, and the enormous dislocations of men and materials in Canada and Europe were all reminders of the way in which the war had changed Canada and the world. Three great empires, the German, the Austrian and the Russian, had fallen; the last to the improbable and disturbing force of Bolshevism. The British Empire had survived but not without severe strain and uncertainty about the future. Borden expressed the feelings of many when he wrote in his diary on Armistice Day: "The world has drifted from its old anchorage and no man can with certainty prophesy what the outcome will be."

The outcome could not be left to fate. Just as the victory in war had required a human enterprise of majestic proportions, so too would a lasting peace demand extraordinary human commitment. Yet, the difficulties were already clear both at home and abroad. The French, the Italians, the British, the Japanese, and other allied nations were staking their claims to parts of the old German and Austrian Empires; and minorities of central Europe were clamouring for the creation of independent states to represent their distinct nationalities. Even Canada had put forth a modest territorial claim: she enquired whether the British would give one of the former German colonies to the United States in exchange for part of the Alaska panhandle. The proposal met with public indifference and, probably, private derision. The Canadian request indicated the peacemaker's greatest problem: there was simply not enough booty to satisfy the voracious appetites of the victor nations. Still, if new territory was not available, what was the reward for victory? With the spectre of Bolshevism and its revolutionary promise of a society of equals haunting the peace conference, the Allied leaders were all the more anx-

ious to find some compensation for their nation's efforts.

In peace as in war, the international and the domestic problems were closely related. The veterans returned expecting a new and better home and often found no work and personal disappointment. Naturally, those at home who had sacrificed also demanded the benefits which the politicians had promised in the darkest days of the war. Some of the demands were straightforward, justifiable and easily met. For example, female suffrage in federal elections was readily granted because, the politicians argued, women had contributed so fully to the war effort. By 1919, then, votes for women, which had seemed a revolutionary concept a few years before the war, were a fact. And like most political changes, female suffrage symbolized a profound social change: the emergence of women in new roles inside and outside the home.

Other changes, however, prompted demands which governments found more difficult to meet. The war machine had been the catalyst for an unprecedented industrial expansion in Canada and for great inflation, partially because of government policy. It has been estimated that the gross income produced by industry increased from $2,417,000,000 in 1914 to $4,383,000,000 in 1919. The most striking advance occurred in the secondary manufacturing sector where gross income produced rose from $390,000,000 in 1914 to $1,120,000,000 in 1919. Although agricultural production had also expanded during this same period, no longer was Canada primarily an agricultural nation. By 1921 twice as many Canadians were employed in nonagricultural pursuits as in agricultural pursuits. The meaning of these statistics was clear to those who lived in Canada through those war years. They saw the face of Canadian cities change dramatically as new plants sprang up, unemployment disappeared and an acute labour shortage developed. This labour shortage brought tens of thousands of women into the work force and drove wages for all to new heights, but profits and the cost of living went even higher. Between 1914 and 1918, wages rose by approximately fifty percent. In the early years of the war, wage increases far surpassed the rise in the price of commodities. This was not true after 1916, however, when the cost of living index rose eighteen percent in 1917, thirteen percent in 1918, and ten percent in 1919. Workingmen saw their gains being rapidly eroded. The potential for post-war disruption was therefore great since the peace which had promised such abundance seemed only to bring new hardship. The disillusionment often expressed

DEDICATED TO THE BOYS OF THE ROYAL AIR FORCE
COME WITH ME IN MY AEROPLANE
WORDS AND MUSIC BY
FLORENCE M. BENJAMIN
ARRANGED BY
JULES BRAZIL
The Anglo-Canadian Music Publishers' Association, Limited
144 VICTORIA STREET, TORONTO:

itself in new intellectual and political forms. Prior to the war, Canadian political rhetoric was notable for its vacuousness and its lack of what might be termed ideological content. As we have seen, most Canadians before 1914 were unconcerned with government, except as it affected their particular corner of their constituency. Faith in the reward for individual effort and in the omnipotence and benevolence of man's creator were the characteristics of nearly all Canadians. The realism, social criticism, and pessimism which had flourished in pre-war Britain and the United States found almost no counterpart in pre-war Canada. But the war and its aftermath had changed all that; for many Canadians, the optimism and faith of the pre-war years were irretrievably shattered by the nihilistic experience of war. The intellectual development of J. S. Woodsworth, the son of a theologically and politically conservative Methodist missionary in the Canadian West, is a good illustration of this change. During the war years, Woodsworth moved from urban missionary work to doubt and through pacifism to socialism. Having left the Methodist Church, Woodsworth became a longshoreman in 1918 on Vancouver's bustling docks. Here, among the immigrants, illiterates, radicals and ordinary citizens who were the lifeblood of the harbour, Woodsworth decided that a revolution would and should come to Canada. The form of the revolution, peaceful or violent, was not yet clear but, in Woodsworth's mind, the evidence he saw in the frustration and anger of the workers was thoroughly convincing. By November 1918, many Canadians had undergone similar, if less dramatic and well-known, revisions in their values.

Canada's leaders therefore faced an awesome task, one made more difficult by the bitter divisions of the war years, by external events and by new intellectual moods. Unfortunately, Sir Robert Borden and Sir Wilfrid Laurier were too tired and too much the symbols of past battles to supply the necessary leadership. They were not alone, however; most Allied leaders shared their liabilities. In his pre-war political career, Borden had shown himself to be tolerant and sufficiently adventurous to try out new ideas. By the end of the war, this spirit had largely disappeared, and in 1919 Borden seemed to lose confidence in his capacity to govern Canada. His interest then shifted to a different arena, to Europe where he thought the Allied leaders were making fundamental decisions about the future of Canada and the world.

   This concentration upon European events and diplomacy

OPPOSITE
Typical cover of a popular song published soon after the end of the First World War.
Metropolitan Toronto Library Board.

The Peace Conference in session in Paris. Borden is seated in the second seat from the end of the table to the right.
Public Archives Canada, C-242.

did not occur immediately. In fact, when Borden was asked to go to Europe in March 1918, he had suggested that he would be "of more use to Canada and to the Empire" at home. Yet two months later, he departed for Europe. "The usual haphazard leavetaking," grumbled Sir George Foster — one of the cabinet ministers who was left without instructions from the "chief." But this was not merely the "usual" departure; this one signified that Borden was no longer the determined leader of December 1917 who had promised to remake the nation. There were probably several factors to account for this altered perception of his role and his loss of interest in domestic matters. First, he was exhausted: the early months of 1918 had brought new resistance to conscription in Quebec and by labour groups. In his own words, Borden was "keyed up to the utmost limit" during this period. By May 1918, a trip to Europe, even with the submarine danger, could seem a pleasant respite from Canadian politics. Secondly, Borden saw that Canada could not endure another war. He also knew that a future war could only arise from Imperial troubles, not from Canadian action itself. It therefore became imperative for Borden and for Canada that the peace should be a lasting one.

Rt. Hon. Sir Robert L. Borden
Con. 1911 - 1917; Unionist 1917 - 1920

Three freighters of standardized design nearing completion at Montreal in 1918. Shipbuilding was one of the Canadian industries that expanded in a spectacular way to meet wartime needs. Ships by the score were built rapidly in old and new shipyards on both coasts and on the Great Lakes. *Public Archives Canada, C-32799.*

Thirdly, Borden realized soon after the election how little his great electoral victory had changed things. Young men still resisted conscription; working men demanding higher wages still walked off their jobs; and businessmen continued to exploit war production to create extraordinary and, to the government, embarrassing profits. Borden, frustrated by the dissension, angered by popular indifference, and concerned for his role in history, began to believe that his more important work would be in the restructuring of the British Empire and the erection of an apparatus that would maintain world peace. In other words, he could serve Canada best by representing her interests in Europe.

Borden knew that when the Canadian people found out the awful truth about the war there would be dissatisfaction and disillusionment of the type that made democratic government difficult and revolutionary change possible. Indeed, Borden himself was profoundly disturbed by what he knew about the war's direction and the needless loss of thousands of Canadian lives. In July 1918 he had warned Lloyd George:

> Mr. Prime Minister, I want to tell you that, if ever there is a repetition of the battle of Passchendaele, not a Canadian soldier will leave the shore of Canada so long as the Canadian people entrust the Government of their country to my hands.

The surest means of preventing further Passchendaeles was to influence Imperial policy and that could best be done in London.

Borden's interest in Imperial questions was not new. During the spring of 1917, he had played a major role in the proceedings of the Imperial War Conference and Imperial War Cabinet. At the Imperial Conference, he had taken the lead in the drafting of "Resolution IX" which asserted the right of the dominions "to an adequate voice in foreign policy and in foreign relations." If the intent of this important resolution were followed, the dominions and the mother country would possess equality in the formulation of Imperial policy. It seemed that Borden had won the concession sought by Canadian statesmen since Confederation. In the 1918 session of the Imperial War Cabinet, Borden raised this newly acquired voice in criticism of the effectiveness of the British war effort, and, more important, his words had an impact: the British war plans for 1919 reflected Borden's trenchant critique as well as British confidence in the excellence of the Canadian Corps.

By late October 1918, however, the collapse of the Ger-

The Prince of Wales receiving an Indian headdress at Banff which he visited in the course of his Canada-wide tour in 1919.
Public Archives Canada, PA-22290.

Suits for Big Boys
Ages 13 to 18 Years

CANADIAN MADE

CANADIAN MADE

Sturdy Suit of Grey Tweed

94-223
Yoke and knife pleat model suit, strongly tailored from Grey Tweed suitings of wool and cotton mixture. Coat has all-round belt, fastening with buckle. Roomy bloomers have strap and buckle at knee. A well-made, serviceable suit at a reasonable price. Sizes 31 to 36 chest measurements, to fit ages 13 to 18 years.
Delivered.. **8.25**

Novelty Suit of Brown Tweed

94-21
Novelty Suit of Brown Tweed wool and cotton mixture. Coat has three fancy pockets and buckle. Full-fashioned strap and buckle bloomers. A suit that always retains dressy appearance. Sizes 31 to 36 chest measurements, to fit ages 13 to 18 years.
Price, delivered **10.5**

Distinctive in Tailoring
Illustrated above

94-225 Smart style Suit of Brown Tweeds in wool and cotton mixture. Note the cleverly-designed coat with three fancy pockets, all-round belt and yoke and pleat back. Bloomers are roomy and finished with strap and buckle. Sizes 31 to 36 chest measurements to fit ages 13 to 18 years.

Price, delivered **10.25**

Smart Grey Tweed Suit
Illustrated above

94-220 This dressy Suit is tailored from neat patterned Grey Tweeds of good-wearing qualities. Materials are of cotton and wool mixture. Coat is well tailored in a popular model. Roomy bloomers have strap and buckle at knee. Sizes 31 to 36 chest measurements to fit ages 13 to 18 yrs.

Price, delivered **9.00**

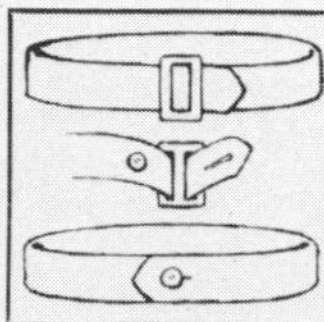

These Suits all Have Our Two-Style Belts For Description See Page 285

Serviceable Tweed

94-221 Brown Suit, made of serviceable Tweed Suitings in wool and cotton mixture. Well tailored in every detail. Coat is made as shown in illustration, back has fancy pleats, as shown in inset. Strap and buckle bloomers. Sizes 31 to 36 chest measurements, to fit ages 13 to 18 years.
Price, delivered...... **9.95**

A Favorite Style

94-224 This suit will give long, satisfactory wear. Materials are closely woven Brown Tweeds of cotton and wool mixture. Carefully tailored in the smart style as shown. Bloomers are full-fitting and finished with strap and buckle at knee. Sizes 31 to 36 chest measurements, to fit ages 13 to 18 years.
Price, delivered............. **9.75**

man front made it clear that these plans were unnecessary. On October 26, Lloyd George asked Borden to come to Britain again, this time to plan for the forthcoming peace conference. Borden's reply to this invitation showed that Canadian nationalism and assertiveness, which were the product of war, would not be lost in peace:

> There is need [Borden wrote] of serious consideration as to representation of the Dominions in the peace negotiations. The press and the people take it for granted that Canada will be represented at the Peace Conference. I appreciate possible difficulties as to representation of the Dominions, but I hope you will keep in mind that certainly a very unfortunate impression would be created and possibly a dangerous feeling might be aroused if these difficulties are not overcome by some solution which will meet the national spirit of the Canadian people.

The British Empire, Borden argued, would best flourish if Britain accepted the right of Canada to take part in world affairs, not only in Imperial councils but also in international organizations.

Borden's proposal was a revolutionary one and it required revision of traditional Imperial practice. "Resolution IX" had promised a reconsideration of the Imperial constitution after the war, but, faced with the reality of peace, many British officials began to draw back from the wartime pledge. British diplomatists in the Colonial Office were horrified to think of Canadians, Australians and New Zealanders, ignorant of the delicacies of diplomacy, planning British policy and at the same time publicly expressing their own opinions. How, they asked, could the Empire have a coherent policy if all its members were allowed to act independently? It was a good question.

When the nations assembled in Paris for the Peace Conference, Canada and the other dominions discovered new resistance to their claims. Furthermore, as part of the British Empire Delegation in Paris, the Dominions found their role a smaller one than they had had in London. Now, the Four Great Powers acted alone and rarely consulted the secondary powers. The Canadians were especially disturbed by the Americans, who objected to separate representation for their neighbour, sometimes in a most patronizing fashion. Why, the Americans asked, should Britain have so much say in the Peace Conference? After all, didn't the Dominions and Britain talk of a common foreign policy? The American view was under-

OPPOSITE
Although the cost of living increased 76 per cent between 1913 and 1919, Eaton's could still offer suits for boys at a top price of $10.50 in the latter year.
Archives, Eaton's of Canada Limited.

standable; to any outsider, the Dominions' arguments were replete with paradox and confusion. After considerable debate, however, the opponents gave way and President Wilson himself worked out the compromise whereby Canada was represented by two delegates at the Peace Conference.

This success encouraged the Canadian delegation to continue its persistence in advancing Canadian claims, as did the awareness that status would be Canada's prize for the victory. As Borden saw it, he and his colleagues had to succeed at Paris. "It was largely a question of sentiment," he wrote in his diary in January 1919, "Canada got nothing out of the war except recognition." Each obstacle heightened Canadian determination, and, backed by a strong public opinion at home and the memories of the success of the Canadian Corps in 1917 and 1918, the Canadians usually got their way. The final achievement was an impressive one. In addition to representation at the Peace Conference, the Canadians gained the right to sign the Versailles Peace Treaty separately, to membership in the International Labour Organization, and most important, to obtain a seat in the League of Nations. Canada had taken a major step into international affairs from which she could not fully retreat even when she wanted to.

When Borden finally returned to Canada in May 1919, he remained confident that his achievements in London and in Paris would be honoured by all Canadians. To be sure, there was some grumbling from Imperialists who feared the talk about separate Canadian status, seeing it — correctly as it turned out — as the harbinger of the death of the British Empire. But on the whole, all evidence suggested that there was satisfaction with the recognition which Canada had attained. There was less contentment, however, with the overall result of the Peace Conference and Borden came to share these doubts. At times, the scrambling for spoils resembled a selfish children's game. Jealousy, hatred and greed were suppressed in the elegance and formality of the public sessions, but in the closed committee rooms they emerged in ugly reality. Wilson, who had arrived in Europe surrounded with the aura of the beneficent peacemaker, left Europe a dying man whose vanity had deeply offended other delegates. The liberal nationalism which had infused Wilsonian rhetoric had proven a dubious principle upon which to reconstruct the European map. Too many of the old problems remained, and there were new ones as well. In fact, it appeared to many that the League of Nations, the great hope for peace in the eyes of millions, might be the agent

for the creation of new wars. Borden saw acute danger in Article X of the League Covenant which provided for the defence of the territory of all member states against external aggression. He pointed out that this article assumed that existing borders were the right borders and that change was neither good nor possible. The continuing turmoil in Europe and elsewhere made such an assumption unrealistic. If Article X remained intact, it might bring Canada into another war in which she had no direct interest. The effect on Canadian public opinion of such a war was too horrible for Borden to contemplate.

There was another compelling reason for Canadian scepticism about the League: the failure of Woodrow Wilson to persuade the American Congress that the United States should join the League. The American absence meant that the North American allies might once again travel on separate paths. This was particularly distressing to Canadians who believed that the entry of the Americans into World War I on the Allied side had signalled a new era in Canadian-American relations. The 1911 campaign slogan, "no truck nor trade with the Yankees," had been quickly forgotten in the euphoria of

Sir Wilfrid Laurier lying in state in the Victoria Memorial Museum, temporary home of the House of Commons, in February 1919.
Public Archives Canada, *C-22355.*

The height of automobile
luxury in 1912: the
Ladybird. A Rolls Royce
Silver Ghost with a
special double limousine
body by Barker, built for
Sir John and Lady Eaton.
*Craven Foundation
Automobile Collection*.

1917, as the Canadians had moved quickly to take advantage of the wartime situation. They had first considered the appointment of an ambassador to handle Canadian business in Washington. In 1917, however, the British would not accept the idea of the Dominions having independent representatives abroad. Canada, nevertheless, did send a special War Mission to Washington which carried out diplomatic functions and was an embassy in all but official status.

The formal relations which were developing reflected new economic, social and cultural ties with the United States. Canadian businessmen looked more towards the south, and American capital moved eagerly towards a friendlier Canadian terrain. The prosperous and urbanized Canadians began to admire and delight in American popular culture which, for generations, their school texts had cavalierly scorned. There was a greater awareness of the similarities rather than of the differences between Canadians and Americans. The vitality, good humour and achievements of Americans were emulated, not ridiculed, and Houdini, the World Series, George M. Cohan, and Lillian Gish were probably as well known in Toronto as in Buffalo.

The new importance of the United States in Canadian life had profound effects upon Canada's view of the world after World War I. More than ever, Canada sought to avoid conflict with the United States and, in particular, to limit Imperial and League of Nations commitments which might bring her into conflict with the United States. For Borden and for his successors as Canadian Prime Ministers, Arthur Meighen and William Lyon Mackenzie King, the major object of Canadian foreign policy was the maintenance of the wartime alliance among the United States, Britain and Canada, not only because the sole threat to Canadian soil lay in an Anglo-American conflict but also because the three Prime Ministers believed that Britain and the United States together represented the greatest force for peace and good in the world. If the League could not guarantee peace then Britain and the United States acting in concert could. Since she understood the Americans better than the British and the British better than the Americans, Canada's proper role was to be a "linchpin," an interpreter and mediator between the United States and Britain. Here she could do the best work for the world, the Empire and herself.

Few statesmen have the opportunity to preside over, much less direct, the reorientation of their nation's foreign policy.

Those who have done so normally win the accolades of the historian, providing that their motives are seen to be honourable. Borden knew this and expected that his achievements in winning Canada a place in world councils and in bringing the United States and Britain closer together would gain him an enduring distinction in national, Imperial and even world history. In a sense he was correct: Canadian historians have generally praised Borden's work in Europe, seeing it as the first major step towards eventual Canadian autonomy. Ironically, Borden, who believed devoutly in the British Empire, would not have approved of many of the later steps taken on the path to autonomy where he had once so boldly led. The "linch-pin," too, was admirable as a conception, but it was very rarely effective. Whenever a crisis occurred in American-British relations, the natural inclination of the leaders of the two countries was to deal directly with each other. Sometimes, as in the days of World War II before Pearl Harbor, Canada was a convenient channel for both the United States and Great Britain, but when the Americans declared war, Canada's intermediary role abruptly ended.

One cannot fault Borden for his deficiencies as a prophet. His greatest failure, however, was his failure to educate the Canadian public in foreign policy. Borden envisaged an active foreign policy for Canada, one in which Canada would play a large role in Imperial councils and in the North Atlantic community. But such an activist policy would require the support and the understanding of a broad, articulate sector of the population, and this Borden's proposed policy never had. There were some, of course, especially among upper-middle class English Canadians, who favoured an activist policy, but these were an exception. Most Canadians were simply unconcerned with foreign policy. Some, particularly French Canadians, were inordinately suspicious of any foreign involvement. By 1924 Borden's dreams of a positive Canadian world role had vanished in the face of indifference and opposition. Paradoxically, it was the war, which had apparently created the opportunity for an international role, that had also disillusioned so many Canadians, turning them inwards. They opted for a better life at home and rejected involvement in the cares of the outside world. It was a gamble for which Canadians paid dearly two decades later.

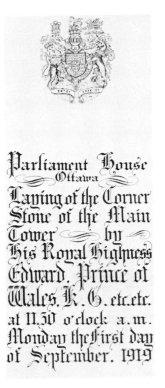

Invitation to the laying of the cornerstone of the Peace Tower. *Metropolitan Toronto Library Board.*

7
A Union Divisible, 1919-1920

Crowds in the streets in Winnipeg at the time of the riots in 1919.
Public Archives Canada, C-26783.

On May 18, 1919, as Sir Robert Borden's ship, the *Aquitania*, set off from England for home, the Canadian Prime Minister wrote in his diary: "I should be very happy to return to Canada were it not for politics." Borden knew that there would be little cheering when he returned; domestic turmoil had overshadowed his achievements in Europe. He was coming back to a profoundly troubled country, obsessed with new problems which had no easy solutions. In April 1919, Thomas White, Borden's confidant and Acting Prime Minister in his absence, had sketched a portrait of seething discontent for the Canadians in Europe. In the West, White warned, "Bolshevism" was rampant and the loyalty of the troops was uncertain. The spirit of revolution was in the air, and the distraught White recommended that a British cruiser show the Imperial colours off the Pacific Coast to intimidate the troublemakers. The Canadians in Paris scoffed at White's suggestion and his analysis; Borden even intimated that White's congenital nervous condition had finally overcome his ability to reason. But within a few weeks, he had come to share White's fears.

The tensions between worker and management, returned soldier and government, poor and rich erupted most dramatically in Winnipeg at the precise moment of Borden's return. What had originated as a dispute over wages and collective bargaining had become a general strike that had the official sanction of the Winnipeg Trades and Labour Council. In the beginning, the strikers had spoken in traditional and practical terms of money, of labour rights and of working hours, but soon they were uttering the rhetoric of revolution with its prophecies of a newer and better world emerging from the overthrow of the old. Their hopes were spurred by the knowledge of successful revolutions in Russia, Hungary and Germany. But there was far more than mere rhetoric in the strikers' complaints; there was genuine outrage at the inequality of Canadian society in 1919. James Winning, the President of the Winnipeg Trades and Labour Council, expressed labour's sense of inequality:

> The other elements of the community never seem to be in want neither in the matter of food, clothing, suitable residence, education, medical and other professional attention, or even recreation, yet Labour is not only never assured but is very often deprived of the essentials of these things.

In Winnipeg, a city of two hundred thousand, destitution and opulence were only a few hundred feet apart, and the propinquity naturally bred both hatred and fear.

Such feelings were not restricted to Winnipeg's working-men in 1919. Since the beginning of the war, Canadian labour had steadily become more organized and more radical. Membership in labour unions had risen from 143,200 in 1915 to 248,900 in 1918 and 378,000 in 1919. As labour's ranks swelled so did its militancy. In 1915 there had been only 62 strikes or lockouts involving slightly more than 11,000 workers. In 1917, there were 158 strikes or lockouts involving over 50,000 workers. Two years later an unprecedented 332 strikes or lockouts occurred which affected almost 150,000 workers. Some major reasons for labour's unprecedented growth are clear. Too many businessmen were too obviously scoundrels, using patriotism to justify low wages while profits and production soared. Moreover, the government often seemed to be an accomplice in these actions. It firmly rejected conscription of wealth and appeared to do very little to halt profiteering. Businessmen had an honoured place in the highest councils, but labour did not even have a voice in the cabinet until 1917. The arrogance of the businessmen-administrators sometimes startled the Prime Minister. Borden, his Labour Minister, Thomas Crothers, and the British Prime Minister Lloyd George all attempted to have fair wage clauses inserted in Imperial Munitions Board contracts in Canada, but the Chairman of the Board, the Canadian businessman Sir Joseph Flavelle, refused to comply on the grounds that "The work people associated with many of these factories would be out of employment were it not for the labour conditions which have been created through these War Orders being executed [in Canada]." What infuriated labour was Flavelle's apparent refusal to apply similar reasoning to company profits. The assets of Flavelle's own business, Wm. Davies Co. Ltd., had more than doubled during the war, almost entirely as a result of the increased export of meat to Great Britain. Flavelle's personal gain during the 1915-1917 period was estimated by a government commission as $1,685,345. Patriotism, labour leaders charged, meant prosperity for the capitalist and sacrifice for the worker.

In 1917, the extent of the sacrifice demanded became greater when the Borden government introduced conscription, thereby breaking a pledge made earlier to labour groups. Labour militants immediately called for a general strike to oppose conscription, but after a heated debate, the Trades and Labour Congress decided to obey the law but to demand that wealth as well as men be conscripted. Wealth was not "con-

scripted," and organized labour's lack of influence in the political system was obvious to all, particularly after labour candidates fared poorly in the 1917 election. Naturally, many workers concluded that the system itself must be changed and the Russian Revolution offered a clear model to many. This was especially true in Western Canada whose labour leaders had always regarded the Eastern dominated Trades and Labour Congress as too conservative.

At the 1918 Trades and Labour Congress convention, Western delegates introduced a series of radical resolutions almost all of which were rejected. After the convention, a caucus of Western delegates began to plan a separate Western labour conference for the next year. Both the rhetoric and the actions of the Westerners frightened the government, and it responded with censorship and, in some cases, repression. This response heightened the radical momentum. When the Western Labour Conference met in Calgary in March 1919, the radicals possessed unquestioned control of the convention. Pointing to the Soviet success, they called for "One Big Union" which, through a general strike, could overwhelm Canada's political and economic establishment. The convention declared

> its full acceptance of the principle of "Proletarian Dictatorship" as being absolute and efficient for the transformation of capitalistic private property to communal wealth, and that fraternal greetings be sent to the Russian Soviet Government, the Spartacans in Germany, and all working class movements in Europe and the world, recognizing they have won first place in the history of the class struggle.

The radicals hoped and the government feared that the next chapter in that history would be written in Canada.

Such was the setting as tens of thousands of Winnipeg workers left their jobs in May 1919 and headed for the streets. At enthusiastic gatherings, the strike leaders exhorted the strikers to stand fast and not to submit to intimidation by their employers. Two Protestant clergymen, J. S. Woodsworth and William Ivens, evoked a vision of God's paradise on earth, using the language of the King James Bible and reflecting the strong tradition of the Social Gospel. Other speakers, however, denounced existing society in angrier tones, employing the seductive logic of Marxism and the eloquent rage of the *Communist Manifesto*. All in all, it was a remarkable event. The war years, the unfulfilled promise of a

OPPOSITE
Joseph W. Flavelle, one of the most noted industrialists and financiers of the Borden era.
Public Archives Canada,
C-23692.

The Borden years saw the beginning of mechanization in farming on the broad expanses of the prairies. Horses, which still provided the power on most farms, began to give way to steam and later to gasoline-powered tractors. One result was an increase in crop yield, since it was no longer necessary to devote part of a farm to raising feed for the horses. On the other hand, tractors and fuel to run them sharply increased cash expenditures. An early example of mechanization: steam tractors breaking virgin prairie in 1917. *Glenbow-Alberta Institute, Calgary, Alberta.*

better life and the coming together of workers in labour unions had led the strikers towards a common understanding which would have been inconceivable before 1914. For over a month the Strike Committee was virtually sovereign in Winnipeg as it took over the functions of protection and welfare that were normally carried out by the government. To the upper-middle class of the city, revolution had come to Winnipeg and its fate was as certain as that of Czar Nicholas. But the traditional leaders were not yet ready to give up or flee.

In the Manitoba Club, a refuge for the city's elite in those stormy days, a defence of the city was planned. A Citizens' Committee of One Thousand was formed to appeal to outside government, to Canadians in general, and especially to those unions which feared the radicalism of the Winnipeg streets. Faced with this demand for action from so many leading Manitobans and fearful of sympathy strikes elsewhere in the nation, the federal government resolved to intervene on the side of established authority. Gideon Robertson, the Minister of Labour and a conservative union leader before 1917, left Ottawa to negotiate with the strikers. He was joined by Arthur Meighen, a Manitoban himself and a close friend of many

Citizens' Committee members. Not surprisingly, Robertson and Meighen soon reached the conclusion that they were witnesses to a revolution whose leaders were not only foreigners but also agents of an international conspiracy. The two cabinet ministers quickly recommended that the leaders be deported, and, within a few days, the Immigration Act was amended to permit deportation without trial. But the discovery that strike leaders were predominantly Anglo-Saxon thwarted this move and embarrassed the government. As a result, a confrontation between government and the strikers became inevitable. It was the government that made the first move.

On Robertson's urging, strike leaders were arrested and the strikers' demands were dismissed as impossible to consider. Tension grew and on June 21, returned soldiers, enraged by the government's attitude towards the strike and by their own situation, took to the streets. The demonstration was illegal, Winnipeg's Mayor Gray had already warned the protesters that force would confront them if they challenged legitimate authority. But the mayor's special police could not cope with the mob. A fateful decision was made when Mayor Gray called for the help of the "Mounties." On horseback the

A stack loader in Alberta in 1919 — primitive by modern standards, but a saver of time and labour. *Glenbow-Alberta Institute, Calgary, Alberta.*

Mounted Police moved up Main Street, passing through the jeering crowd and then returning to face their foe. In this dramatic setting, Mayor Gray read the Riot Act but the crowd failed to disperse. The "Mounties" moved forward and within minutes shooting broke out. In a moment one striker died, dozens were wounded, Winnipeg trembled.

The violence frightened the government as much as the strikers. The government reacted with further harshness: membership or participation in a seditious organization was made a crime whose punishment was twenty years in a penitentiary. The strikers had had enough; moreover, they knew that in any test of physical strength they were certain losers. They returned to work, their unions and their dreams shattered. Yet the memory of those heady spring days in Winnipeg played a part in later Canadian history. Radicals of the thirties and the sixties remembered the strikers with admiration and the repression with anger. Also, the socialist government of Manitoba and the socialist party founded in the 1930s by

Threshing in the steam tractor era, a familiar sight for a generation. The modern combine has banished it from the prairie scene.
Public Archives Canada, C-6034.

strike leader J. S. Woodsworth owe much to the thoughts and actions of 1919.

The tragedy at Winnipeg was the result of misperception. The strikers had underestimated the government's strength and the government had exaggerated the strikers' power and purpose. The government's confusion is nevertheless understandable; there were certainly notions of revolution and rumours of conspiracies everywhere. The political landscape which Borden confronted upon his return was most unfamiliar terrain for the veteran statesman, and he trod it with hesitation, fear and clumsiness. One of the most striking changes had occurred in February 1919 when Sir Wilfrid Laurier died, a gallant warrior for almost half a century of Canadian politics. His death brought forth nostalgia for those simpler and better times at the turn of the century. Perhaps it was because the Unionists thought that the passions of 1917 had died with Laurier that they organized a majestic state funeral for the Liberal leader. But Laurier's friends had not forgotten the battle two years earlier. As Sir Wilfrid's funeral cortège passed through Ottawa's silent streets, Charlie Murphy, Laurier's old lieutenant, was heard to say: "Do you think we can trust the buggers with his body?"

While the old wounds still festered, new ones appeared. For the Unionists one of the most irritating was a militant farmers' movement. In 1917 the entry of Thomas Crerar into the Union Government had signified the commitment of farm leaders to conscription and to Union Government. During the campaign, the Unionists paid a further price for farm support: exemption from conscription for farmers and their sons. In March 1918 the German offensive led the government to cancel this exemption and thereby create a sense of betrayal among Canadian farmers. Crerar became most uncomfortable in his role as Minister of Agriculture as his old friends harassed him publicly and privately. When the war ended, the decrease in demand for agricultural produce and the continuing inflation heightened agrarian discontent. While the markets for wheat and other commodities dried up and their prices fell, farm implements became more expensive. The government, still dependent on the tariff for much of its income, refused to lower the tariff, an action which would have considerably reduced the price of implements and other goods which the farmer needed. City dwellers, fully aware of the farmer's wartime booty, took little pity on him. The farmer, it seemed, stood alone. With the Unionists "betraying" their farm supporters and the Liberals still tainted by the stands they took in 1917, the farmers of the Canadian West and Ontario lingered in a state of political limbo. To the government it seemed more a state of confusion: some farmers demanded the lifting of wartime controls and others urged new state control of agriculture. Crerar found the conflicting currents too strong and cast himself adrift from the Unionists in early June 1919. Thomas White's 1919 budget had not lowered tariffs significantly and had given Crerar a pretext for resignation. In reality, Crerar, who had continued to write most of his letters on United Grain Growers' stationery, had to leave because Union Government had become anathema to Western agricultural interests, Crerar's primary focus of loyalty.

Whatever the motivation, Crerar's resignation intensified the politicization of the farmers' movement. Political independence gained a new respectability and adherence to the Union Government attracted increasing scorn. Informal agrarian organizations or movements congealed into political parties, although the farmers themselves were reluctant to call these new entities parties. Provincial governments like that of Saskatchewan which had supported the Unionists in 1917 quickly cut their ties. A farmers' party which had at first seemed risible, became a reality, as other Western Members of Parliament joined Crerar as independents. Soon, the group dubbed themselves the Progressive Party and adopted as their platform "the New National Policy." This platform merited neither the portentous title nor the Unionist charge that it was revolutionary. On the whole, the New National Policy was a familiar litany of the farmers' complaints mixed with a few new notions borrowed from American agrarian radical movements. It called for free trade in agricultural machinery and certain other goods, nationalization of railway companies, and strict controls over natural resource development. Recommended political innovations included initiative and referendum, female suffrage, prohibition and civil service reform. The program may have been familiar but it was nonetheless an effective rallying cry. In the summer of 1919 a farmers' candidate decisively won a federal by-election in Saskatchewan and struck fear into the hearts of Western Liberals and Unionists. Even more shocking was the victory of the United Farmers of Ontario in the Ontario provincial election in October 1919. The "UFO" itself was surprised; it even lacked a leader to become premier. Within a few days, however, E. C. Drury emerged as leader and became the only third party premier in Ontario's history.

Enthusiasm swept the West when the bastion of the hated Eastern "interests," the province of Ontario, fell to the agrarian assault. Thomas B. Costain, then a shrewd Canadian journalist and later a prominent novelist, wagered that the chance of a federal farmers' government was "at least fifty-fifty." In late 1919 the tide seemed irresistible as old politicians scurried for refuge. But the agrarian revolt was short-lived, and Costain lost his bet.

Two more provinces, Alberta and Manitoba, did elect farmers' governments, and in 1921 the Progressives did become the second party in the Canadian House of Commons. Within five years, however, the impetus behind the farmers' movement was lost, never to be recovered. The movement was as much a symbol of the general political and emotional turmoil which followed the war as it was an expression of agrarian dissent. So, too, was the labour movement. Although some historians have expressed scepticism about the alliance between the farmers and labour in the early days of the United Farmers Government in Ontario, there was, in fact, a genuine commonality of interest between the two groups. Both farmers and workers had been excited by the wartime promises of politicians, clergymen and public leaders, but both realized these promises were not and probably never would be fulfilled. After the war, the federal government's main concern was to get the nation back on its old tracks. But the farmers and labourers wanted new tracks, ones which led towards different goals. In short, these two social groupings were alienated from the political system. They felt that their position within post-war society was unsatisfactory and that it did not recognize their unique contribution to the nation. Dissent and even violence were the inevitable product of this frustration.

In another sense, however, the agricultural and labour protest movements were fundamentally dissimilar. The difference is revealed in their respective programs. Much of the farmers' New National Policy has an archaic ring to a modern reader. There is a quaint simplicity to many of its planks. In terms of modern categories of political thought, the New National Policy is at once utopian, reactionary, progressive and romantic; it is a baffling political collage, a hodgepodge of profundity and nonsense. While it is true that many of labour's demands were also utopian, the essence of the labour platform is surprisingly contemporary. Many planks in the platform are political issues today, and such concepts as collective bargaining, unemployment insurance, minimum wages, and health insurance are an integral part of modern Canadian society. It is here that the real distinction between agrarian and labour dissent becomes apparent. While calling themselves "progressives," the agrarian protesters too often tended to base their analysis on the past and to ignore clear trends in post-war society. This is clearly manifested in the outlook of their spokesmen.

Thomas Crerar, for example, was a consistent advocate of reduced state powers in the Unionist cabinet. The "positive state" which wartime needs had created was repugnant to him. Crerar's resistance to social welfare schemes as a Liberal cabinet minister during World War II startled many, but it was not at all inconsistent with his earlier "progressive" incarnation. Another example is W. C. Good, an Ontario farm leader, who urged the state to adopt the single tax along with various other nostrums for the nation's ills culled from diverse sources. But it is William Irvine's 1920 study of *The Farmer in Politics* which best illustrates the inherent weakness of the agrarian protest movement. Irvine, a Methodist clergyman of British birth, had been an early advocate of direct political action by farmers. In his book he gave the reasons for his stand. The rural life, Irvine claimed, bred a stock most suitable for democracy. The corruption of Canadian politics could be

directly traced to the lack of farmers in politics. Looking at past Canadian Parliaments, Irvine found few farmer members. The result of this, Irvine argued, was a government controlled by big Eastern commercial and industrial interests that had little concern for the farmer's lot. There is some truth in this, but most of Irvine's analysis is superficial and misleading.

What Irvine failed to notice was that the farmers' problems arose from the rapid decline of their relative position within society. As late as 1891 Canada had been approximately two-thirds rural, but by 1911 the nation was forty-four percent urban and by 1921 almost fifty percent urban. Moreover, many of the rural settlements had become dependent upon nearby urban centres and were inextricably linked with them through the street railways, and increasingly, through the automobile. For years, farmers' sons had been leaving the farms to seek what they thought was a more prosperous existence in the industries of Toronto, Montreal, Halifax and very often, the United States. Entire small communities disappeared leaving abandoned fields and barns as testimony to a once vital community. While the farm population remained static, the number working in factories and living in cities spiralled upwards. If anything, the maldistribution of political constituencies gave the rural areas more influence than their population warranted. The trend was irreversible; Canada's future would be urban and industrial.

The agrarian protest was therefore defensive, eclectic, and notably deficient in analysis. It was the manifestation of a loss of power by the farming community. On the other hand, the labour disorders were symbols of vitality and of the emergence of a new locus of power within Canadian society. Labour union membership had swollen from 166,200 at the beginning of the war to 378,000 in 1919, and although membership later declined, the independent power of labour did not. The agrarian leaders eventually fell into line behind the two old parties, normally the Liberals. Some agrarian radicals, like William Irvine and Agnes MacPhail, became founding members of the Cooperative Commonwealth Federation. The farmers remained a potent political force, and they continued to dominate Western provincial governments for many more decades. But the vision of the New National Policy proved a mirage. The Winnipeg strikers' dream of a worker's paradise also faded, but the labour movement and socialism played an increasingly greater role in national politics, and the possibility of the organization of Canadian society in a socialist framework continues to animate many Canadians today.

One cannot accuse Borden and Union Government of failing to recognize farm and labour discontent at an early stage. Farm and labour interests were more highly represented in the Union Government than in any previous one. Also, the Union Government had promised and, to a certain extent, had given the kind of progressive government which farmers and workers claimed to want. The franchise for women, the abolition of titles, the nationalization of railways, prohibition, the recognition of collective bargaining, and several other measures seemed to be of the type which would commend themselves to either farm or labour groups or to both. But these gains had only whetted the appetite for more. Paradoxically, by 1919 the most vigorous opposition to Unionism came from the areas of its greatest strength in 1917 and the least visible dissent came from Quebec.

Labour and farm unrest was present in Quebec, but, from the government's point of view, its manifestations were far more acceptable. There was a march of French-Canadian farmers on Ottawa, but, on the whole, the protest movement was weak. The labour history of Quebec in this period is more interesting. The Catholic Church had taken the leadership in the social reform movements which emerged in Quebec. A 1915 strike at Thetford Mines, which had been organized by a militant union, led the Church to form a Catholic union. From this beginning, the movement against international unions and for Catholic unions grew quickly in the province, as French-Canadian leaders endorsed the Catholic unions as more suitable for their society. The socialism advocated by many national and international unions would destroy the fabric of French-Canadian society; therefore, secular unions could not be tolerated. And although significant elements in the Church deplored the poverty of much of French Canada and hoped to end it, they could never consider socialism as a palliative for deprivation. All of this was most reassuring to Borden and his colleagues, and, as one might expect with politicians, they gave the credit for Quebec's placidity to the provincial government of Sir Lomer Gouin.

Borden had always thought highly of Gouin, a Liberal in name but conservative in every other sense. Gouin's mastery of Quebec politics was well established, and his demeanor after the federal election of 1917 had won him widespread approval in English Canada. When J. N. Francoeur, a Liberal backbencher in the Quebec Assembly, introduced a motion in January 1918 which contemplated the end of Confederation as a possible reaction to the Unionist victory, Gouin had spoken eloquently against the motion and in defence of Confederation urging French Canadians not to turn their backs on Canada but to "struggle fearlessly against the passing storm" and "labour ceaselessly and untiringly to develop and maintain the Canadian Confederation." When rioting against the enforcement of conscription broke out in Quebec in the spring of 1918, Gouin came down quickly on the side of law and order. Gouin, it seemed to Borden, stood for order and patriotism; he could become a valuable ally for the Unionists.

Borden first asked Gouin to enter federal politics in May 1918. At that time Gouin declined, saying he was too old, an answer that must have startled Borden who was six years older than Gouin. In 1919, Hugh Graham, now Lord Atholstan, and James Calder persuaded Borden to meet with Gouin once again. The times seemed propitious. The clear threat to established order in the streets of Winnipeg had shocked Gouin as it had Borden. Moreover, Sir Wilfrid Laurier's death early in 1919 had removed Quebec's most eloquent spokesman in Ottawa. Of the likely successors to Laurier in the Liberal Party, none was a French Canadian. Furthermore, French Canada's future seemed uncertain in a Liberal Party committed to social reform, and Mackenzie King, one of the leading candidates for Laurier's post, promised such a party. Realizing Gouin's situation, Borden sent Calder to meet Gouin and to tell him that "the welfare of our country" required the ending of Quebec's isolation. One way in which the isolation could be ended was the entry of prominent Quebec politicians such as Gouin into the Union Government. The report which Calder submitted to Borden suggested that Gouin was sympathetic to the tenor of this appeal. Gouin proposed that Borden should come to Quebec and meet him and three other prominent Quebec politicians, Jacques Bureau, Rodolphe Lemieux and Ernest Lapointe.

Borden decided to make a holiday of the occasion by taking a leisurely St. Lawrence cruise. The first stop was at Trois-Rivières where Borden met with the gregarious Jacques Bureau who was friendly but evasive. His party then continued on to Rivière du Loup where he spoke with Ernest Lapointe, and then to Quebec where he talked with his old friend and Quebec's Lieutenant Governor, Sir Charles Fitzpatrick. The final and most important destination was Murray Bay, the elegant watering place for Montreal's elite, and incidentally, for the prominent Taft family from the United

States. It must have brought Borden some pleasure when he and Sir Henry Drayton defeated Sir Lomer Gouin and the former American President, William Howard Taft, in a game of golf. The conversation with Sir Lomer and his fellow Liberal, Rodolphe Lemieux, was much less satisfactory, although both were to a large degree, sympathetic towards Borden's aims. Gouin admitted that he feared the new Liberal leader might endorse free trade and social programs which were unpopular in Quebec. But, Sir Lomer added, the Union Government remained intensely unpopular in Quebec. There might not be open protest, but in the polling booth, the French Canadian would never place his mark beside a Unionist candidate. The bilingual school issue in Ontario, conscription, the presence of the Liberals who deserted Laurier in the Union Government, all of these things made the thought of entering that government quite impossible for French-Canadian politicians. Atholstan, a confidant of both Gouin and Borden, probably did not exaggerate when he told Borden that even Gouin, the political master of the province, could not win a federal seat if he decided to join the Union Government. The St. Lawrence journey was the desperate attempt of a government in serious trouble to save itself. After the collapse of the negotiations with Gouin, Borden knew that the government's days were numbered, and he looked forward to his own departure from a political world that was neither agreeable nor comprehensible.

The attempted alliance with Gouin, a French Canadian, a conservative and a friend of the "interests," symbolized a fundamental shift in the outlook of English-Canadian Unionists. In 1917 Union Government meant not only conscription but also a broad program of reform. Experiment and innovation were encouraged and promised. There would be, to use a Unionist phrase of 1917, a new era in Canada which would build upon Canada's past and present but would be infinitely richer in all aspects of human affairs. Even the cynical Clifford Sifton could imagine that the disappearance of poverty, disease and a myriad of other social and political ills required only decent and intelligent national leadership. In the year and a half after 1917, this confidence in the essential simplicity of change was lost; indeed, events like the Winnipeg General Strike had bred a deep fear of change. For example, J. W. Dafoe, an ardent supporter of the reform program of the Unionists, was horrified by what he saw in the streets outside his *Manitoba Free Press* editor's office in

OPPOSITE
Lady Borden, always an attractive subject for the photographer, in her middle years.
Public Archives Canada,
C-49529.

the spring of 1919. There was a mindless, alien quality in the demands and the actions of the strikers that could not be tolerated no matter how legitimate the grievances were. If the strike represented the direction of change, then change must be stopped.

Men like Sifton, Dafoe, Rowell and Borden were political Whigs, similar to the aristocrat reform leaders in early nineteenth century Britain who consciously played two roles. On the one hand, they presented themselves as the friend of reform, adding immense respectability to any cause by their support; on the other hand, they worked to assure that reform would never become revolution. Dafoe, Borden and other Unionist reformers similarly recognized that the benefits of industrialization and prosperity must accrue to the workers, to the farmers and to the disadvantaged in general. At the same time, they never lost their belief that Canadian society was fundamentally healthy and that the redistribution of national wealth must be carried out through consent, not confiscation, and within the political system, not in the streets. The post-war troubles had an immediate impact, and the "birth of a new era" suddenly aborted. And if the present was marked by fear, the future would be marked by caution and cynicism.

The automobile first began to be widely used during the years when Borden was Prime Minister. In 1910 there were only 5890 passenger cars in Canada; in 1920 there were 251 945. In the same period more than thirty companies attempted to produce automobiles in Canada. This 1912 Atlas car was marketed by the Brockville-Atlas Company, of Brockville, Ontario. It had turned out its first car in 1911, enjoyed some success, but was forced to suspend operations in 1915, owing to shortages arising from the war.
Craven Foundation Automobile Collection.

8
Borden Retires

Sir Robert in retirement: on board ship in 1930, aged 76.

WITHIN A YEAR of the war's end, the Winnipeg strikers, the Ontario farmers and the French Canadians combined in an unlikely alliance that assured the imminent collapse of the Union Government and the end of the political career of its creator, Sir Robert Borden. His last year as Prime Minister was a struggle to permit a respectful interment for Unionism and a graceful departure for himself. His foes were impatience and exhaustion, and the battle was not easy. No successor was apparent and no convenient moment for resignation could be found. Without conscription as a unifying issue, the Union Government lost its *raison d'être* and the coalition of Liberals, independents and Conservatives rapidly disintegrated. Rather than uniting the Unionists, reconstruction problems served to expose the Unionists' internal divisions. Long after Borden expressed his desire to leave political life, he lingered on as a "lame duck" prime minister. The consequences were unfortunate for Unionism, for Borden and for Canada. They were, however, most beneficial to a resurgent Liberal Party under the leadership of Laurier's successor, William Lyon Mackenzie King.

A national Liberal leadership convention in August 1919 had chosen King as leader and, at King's insistence, had adopted a reformist platform. These events greatly hastened the reconciliation of the Liberal factions of 1917. The effects were noticed immediately: within Parliament, the Liberal Unionists were increasingly isolated as many of their 1917 supporters returned to their former allegiance or rallied to the new Progressives' side. As the Liberal Unionists departed, the Union Government became more Conservative, and the Conservative majority hurried to cast off the Unionist mantle that had enshrouded the party since 1917. The declining fortunes of Unionism led to angry confrontations in caucus and in cabinet meetings. Why, the Conservative Unionists asked, should the Liberal Unionists continue to receive government patronage when their loyalty was so manifestly weak? Moreover, why should Liberals like Newton Rowell and James Calder occupy senior cabinet posts and formulate important government policy when their political bases had disappeared? Such questions were not easily answered, and each concession to Conservative opinion speeded the departure of the remaining Liberals. Since Borden found Rowell, Calder and other Liberal Unionists personally and ideologically congenial, and the Tory loyalists like Rogers personally and politically repugnant, he deplored the situation. He accepted that

Unionism was dead, but he wanted to ensure the perpetuation of its major accomplishments and to protect those Liberal Unionists who had stood by him but were now becoming political orphans, welcome neither in Liberal nor in Conservative ranks. Borden did his best, but in early December 1919 his doctor told him he could do no more. He was on the brink of complete nervous collapse.

Almost immediately Borden told his colleagues of his intention to resign. To the surprise of many journalists who had heard the grumbling of the backbencher, the caucus refused to let Borden step down. Liberal Unionists knew that Borden was their protector and that a future leader would likely abandon them. The Conservatives, too, begged Borden to stay on, primarily because they did not see any alternative. There was, nevertheless, one cabinet minister who refused to join the chorus pleading with Borden to remain—Arthur Meighen. The partisan and candid Meighen warned that delaying Borden's departure would only compound the Unionist confusion. He was correct, but his advice was not heeded. Borden remained under a preposterous compromise; he would publicly announce his intention to retire but state that, instead of an immediate resignation, he would take a long vacation and then temporarily resume his duties as Prime Minister until a new leader could be found. On January 2, 1920, the announcement made, Borden left on a southern cruise with Lord Jellicoe.

The press was astonished; the Liberals delighted. The Unionists' woe and indecision became the butt of popular jokes, even among those thought to be friends. In one particularly nasty exchange, Sir John Willison wrote to Sir Clifford Sifton:

You have no doubt heard why the ship that Borden was to christen at Halifax slipped into the water before the ceremony could be performed. It could not wait for Borden to make up his mind.

With characteristic acidity, Sifton replied:

I had not heard that joke about Borden but it is extremely good. He will go down to posterity (as far as he goes) as Robert the Unready.

Sifton, who prided himself on his acute political antennae not on his loyalty to friends, proved by his comment that he

199

lacked both. It was not Borden who was unready but rather his party. In the party's view, Borden had to remain leader even if he were leader in name only. The view was understandable, but it destroyed Borden's hopes for a graceful departure and simply postponed the Unionists' inevitable decision. Winter passed and spring came with Borden still absent from Canada. As he rested in the southern United States, letters from Ottawa arrived that regularly detailed the exhaustion of the ministers and the inability of the Unionists to agree on their future course. For Borden, such news did not make the thought of returning home a pleasant one, but true to his promise, he came back to Ottawa on May 12 to resume his work once more. His resolve was short-lived: after a brief bout with the political realities, Borden and his doctors agreed that he had to resign whatever the consequences. On Dominion Day, 1920, Borden announced his irrevocable decision to the final caucus of the Unionist party.

One thing was clear: Borden's successor and a party platform had to be found immediately; there was no time for a convention. As Borden's last service to his party, he presided over the choice of the new leader. He began by polling both the cabinet and the caucus on their favourites. As one might have expected, the Unionists did not vote in unison. The predominantly Conservative caucus voted decisively for Arthur Meighen whose highly partisan attacks on Mackenzie King and vigorous defences of government policy had delighted the Tory backbenchers. The cabinet, on the other hand, was aware that Meighen's sarcasm and candour were more popular in the House of Commons than in the country, and it almost unanimously recommended Sir Thomas White. Borden, who had rarely listened to backbenchers before and had no intention of doing so now, immediately called on White, who had resigned from the Cabinet in August 1919. But White had wearied of political wars, his health was poor, and he feared defeat. Thus, he refused to accept the Governor General's invitation to form a government. After browbeating some of his colleagues to remain in the new government, Borden announced that Arthur Meighen would be his successor, and on July 10, 1920, the forty-six-year-old Meighen became the leader of the new National Liberal-Conservative Party and the ninth Prime Minister of Canada.

Borden's active political career came to an end with his resignation. The press announcements reporting the retirement were generally kind, but few of them suggested that he would be remembered as one of Canada's great Prime Ministers. In a 1921 book, the journalist Augustus Bridle summed up the contemporary opinion of Borden:

> Canada never before had a mediocrity of such eminence;
> a man who without a spark of genius devoted a high talent
> to a nation's work so well that he just about wins a niche
> in our Valhalla — if we have one. It was the war that almost
> finished Borden and it was the war that made him.

Journalists recognized that, whatever their limitations, Borden and his governments had left a lasting imprint upon Canada and he would not be quickly forgotten. In 1901 when the Conservative Party chose an almost unknown Halifax lawyer as its temporary leader, the event was reported on the inner pages of the newspaper. The "temporary" leader's departure almost two decades later made front page headlines across Canada. This is an indication of Borden's important role and of the way in which the country had changed. During the Borden years, national politics had come to matter so much more than they had at the turn of the century.

When Borden became Conservative leader in 1901, Canada was a nation of seven provinces with a population of 5.3 million and a gross national product that had just reached one billion dollars. Its industry, its literature, its art, and its interests were all limited in scale and scope. There were no motor cars confidently manoeuvring through crowded city streets, and Canada's first manned flight was still several years away. There was but one transcontinental railway, and, for much of that railway's length, settlement extended only a few miles from the main tracks. The Canadian West was only a few years past Louis Riel and the buffalo hunters, and the first wave of immigrants had barely begun to build their sod huts on the prairies.

Canada before the Great War was a land of little introspection. While a healthy optimism suffused its literature, popular magazines and political oratory, this mood reflected adolescent faith more than a mature understanding of the nation's circumstances and possibilities. Canadians knew neither themselves nor their nation very well. In general, the individual Canadian's vision was restricted to the neighbourhood, the town and the countryside in which he dwelt. Few imagined that any national event could have a profound impact on their daily lives. Almost none dreamed of a European

As part of his post-retirement activities, Borden offered his seasoned views on Canadian constitutional development at the University of Toronto in the Marfleet Lectures of 1921.
Varsity, *October 7, 1921. University of Toronto Archives.*

SIR ROBERT BORDEN SPEAKS IN CONVOCATION HALL

Traces the Romantic Story of Canadian Constitutional Development

VARSITY GRADUATE HELPED TO MAKE HISTORY

Sir Robert Borden Explains the Steps by which the Dominion has Risen to Nationhood

Varsity Oct. 7/21

The first of the Marfleet Lectures was delivered by Sir Robert Borden on Wednesday, October 6th, in Convocation Hall. The audience was exceedingly representative in its character, including such prominent personalities as Sir Thomas White and Hon. N. W. Rowell, and many others.

The former Prime Minister was accompanied on the platform by Sir Robert Falconer, who, in a few well-chosen sentences, described the character and history of the Marfleet foundation, and then presented the distinguished lecturer to the audience. The lecture was occupied in covering Canadian constitutional development up to Confederation, necessitating a rapid survey of the French concepts of government prior to the conquest; the efforts made by the British Government to introduce English methods and principles of law; the difficulties which were intensified by the advent of the U.E.L. after the American Revloutionary War; the paternalistic conception of its responsibility which was held by the Colonial Office, with the resulting friction and misunderstandings; the enlightened policy outlined by Lord Durham; the statesmanlike work of Poulett-Thompson in attempting to harmonise apparently irreconcilable interests; the concurrent growth in England and Canada of what are now known as "democratic" principles; the gradual assertion of the peoples in both countries of the right of responsible government; the Parliamentary deadlock which brought about the agreement of Brown and Macdonald (politically and personally as far apart as the poles) to sink their differences in an effort to nd a way out of the impasse; and lastly, the crowning result of Confederation.

The lecture, while on a serious constitutional problem, was lightened by touches of humour which added pungency to points which the lecturer intended to drive home, while the claim that in Canada is to be found one of the highest forms of democracy extant was appreciated by the audience.

The strictures on the attitude of the British Government toward Canadian aspiration in those early days, while somewhat severe, were not unjust, emphasizing as they did the practical impossibility of ruling a proud and self-respecting people

It must be stated, very frankly, that VARSITY was disappointed in so far as the size of the audience was concerned. When we say that Convocation Hall was not quite two-thirds filled on the occasion of such a lecture by a former Prime Minister of the Dominion, there is a self-evident reproof to those who could have been present but were not.

THE SECOND LECTURE

The second of the Marfleet Lectures dealt with the period from Confederation to the Great War.

Sir Robert Borden pointed out that the many judicial interpretations of the B.N.A. formed a body of precedent and tradition of high constitutional importance. In it, there is no formal attempt to define the relations between the Canadian and British Governments and thus there was evolved a gradual growth of custom and convention. In 1887, the first Colonial Conference was held, and this was purely consultative. At that time there was no conception of relation with the colonies other than as subordinates.

The next step in Canadian self-consciousness was the calling of a conference by Canada with Australia and New Zealand to discuss submarine cables and other matters of common interest.

At the Jubilee of 1897, a conference of Prime Ministers was called; and again at the Coronation of King Edward in 1902, but with the addition of other Ministers to assist the Prime Ministers. On this occasion it was moved that conferences should be held every four years.

It should be noticed that none of these conferences was with the British Government, but with one of its Departments.

Imperial Conference

In 1905 a step forward was made by Mr. Lyttleton, Colonial Secretary, when he sent a letter to all the Dominion Prime Ministers suggesti,g that the Colonial Conference should be transformed into an Imperial Council. With the exception of Canada all the Dominions approved the suggestion, and after certain objections had been met, Canada also agreed to the principle.

The first Imperial Conference therefore

conflict that would snuff out the lives of over sixty thousand Canadians. The thought was both too horrible and too ridiculous to contemplate.

By 1920, the thought had become a profound and sad memory. The fury of the Great War had ended forever the sense that all that mattered happened within a few miles of home and the belief that the young Canadian nation faced no future tragedies. But it was not only the intellectual landscape that had changed; political, economic and social patterns were also fundamentally altered. The heart of the prewar political system, patronage, had not endured its conflict with "public interest" during the War. The appointments which were previously made by the federal Members of Parliament were now largely in the hands of an independent civil service commission. As a result, the old style relationship between a member and his constituency could not be maintained; a politician no longer survived on patronage alone. In the words of an acute political observer, J. W. Dafoe, the Union Government experience had "brought to a definite close . . . the era of the Great Parties." The spirit of the Unionist movement had passed with the war, "but it [had] left the old traditional party system in ruins." In 1920 with a third party ruling Ontario and threatening to rout Liberalism and Unionism in the West, the political outlook for Canada had never seemed so uncertain.

The change in the Canadian economy during Borden's years of power was equally great and can be measured more precisely. The 1910 gross national product of $2,235,000,000 had become $5,529,000,000 ten years later. Most of this amazing growth had occurred in the manufacturing and service sectors of the economy. In 1910, agriculture production equalled $509,000,000; manufacturing production, $508,000,000; and services, $752,000,000. By 1920, agricultural production had risen to $1,073,000,000; manufacturing to $1,335,000,000; and services to $1,953,000,000. More important for the average Canadian, average wage rates had more than doubled during this ten year period. Although workers complained loudly about their circumstances in 1919 and 1920, over the entire decade their economic position had improved. And even these figures, striking though they are, do not reflect significant structural changes in the Canadian economy: the expanded role of the state, the large number of women in the work force, the imposition of the income tax, and the redistribution of income caused by high wartime profits and wages. One of the most influential changes probably escaped the notice of most Canadians. In 1911, the value of exports to the United Kingdom was $147,182,000 (current dollars) and to the United States, $100,770,000; in 1920 the respective figures were $343,217,000 and $581,408,000. The figures for imports were more dramatic. In 1911, Canada imported $113,352,000 from Britain and $319,942,000 from the United States; in 1920, she imported $231,488,000 from Britain and an extraordinary $921,235,000 from the United States.

Trade patterns might be reversed but a shift in foreign investment has a great degree of permanence. In 1914, British investment in Canada amounted to seventy-two percent of all foreign investment. By 1921, American investment roughly equalled British investment, and the wartime personal and institutional connections between the United States and Canada assured that the flow from the south would not halt. Also, this American investment was unlike British investment since it tended to reflect itself in the ownership of Canadian firms rather than in loans to them. Ironically, Borden whose party slogan in 1911 had been "no truck nor trade with the Yankees" had opened the forty-ninth parallel more widely than any Prime Minister since Confederation.

As one might expect, these economic changes had profound social implications. A nation that had been predominantly agrarian and sixty-two percent rural in 1901 had become urban and industrial two decades later. Even those areas that remained rural according to the 1921 census definition were now more closely integrated with the cycle of urban life. Several technological innovations were primarily responsible for this. The gramophone brought the voice of Caruso and the songs of George M. Cohan to the farmer's parlor. There was also the "miracle of moving pictures" available to all but the more isolated communities. During the war years, the "movies" had provided an escape from the world's cares and had made Douglas Fairbanks, Lillian Gish, Lionel Barrymore, and Canada's own Mary Pickford familiar to and admired by millions of Canadians. Popular culture became less a reflection of folk or local tradition, and more international, technical, and distant. The social psychological impact of Hollywood, its stars and mass culture is difficult to analyze, but few would suggest that the effect was small.

The rising real incomes brought these technological luxuries to the expanding middle class, and in many cases, to

the Canadian working class. There was, however, one fairly common luxury that the worker could rarely afford: the automobile. Despite its cost, the automobile had revolutionized urban life by 1921 and the migration of the middle class to the suburbs was underway. Ontario had 144,804 motor vehicles registered in 1919; five years earlier, there had been merely 31,724. The province that ranked second in registrations was Saskatchewan with 56,855, a measure of the wheat farmer's prosperity and of the value of the automobile in linking the lonely prairie farm with the nearby town. In all of the provinces, the automobile had become such a common sight by 1920 that horses were undisturbed and children unexcited by its presence.

Not surprisingly, this sudden rush of technological innovation altered the tasks of leadership and the nature of government. Industrialization in Canada as elsewhere had created a somewhat disordered society that lacked the cohesion of pre-industrial society; the ties binding individuals to one another appeared to have broken down. Movements then arose which urged the restoration of the social control achieved in societies of smaller scale through community sanc-

Sir Robert and Lady Borden with a group of Canadians at the League of Nations in Geneva in 1930. They include (on the left) Dr. W. A. Riddell and Norman Robertson, and (with cane) the Hon. Philippe Roy, then Canada's Minister Plenipotentiary to France.

tion. Prohibition was one such attempt to reinvigorate family life and to restore order through the use of the physical power of the state. Groups like the prohibitionists argued that in the new industrial society, it was the state rather than the neighbours that must prevent the individual from antisocial behaviour.

Yet these hopes were bedevilled by the same new technology which appeared to make them possible. The improvements in communications might permit a closer link between the national politician and the individual citizen, but they also heightened the individual's appreciation of the flaws of national leadership. The citizen became more aware of inequality and of goods and services that others possessed but he did not. How could this criticism be countered? How could these new demands be satisfied? There were no clear answers to these crucial questions, and both the purpose and the principles of politics were in doubt.

Borden knew when he resigned that he had neither diagnosed nor found the prescription for the ills of modernization. His efforts had received little reward and he feared they would soon be forgotten. Naturally, there was self pity. Borden ended his memoirs with a 1921 diary quotation that had obvious implications for his own position:

> The Government of M. Venizelos [of Greece] has been defeated, which astonishes me, because he did so much for his country at the Peace Conference. But such things will happen. Democracy is always ungrateful, forgetful and neglectful. I am very happy to have given up my public duties and to have retired from public life.

This cynicism, however, should not stand as the epitaph for Borden's political career.

If Borden did not achieve what he and his countrymen had hoped, he had still done more than most leaders in those difficult times. He had seen the pitfalls in growth, affluence and industrialization at an early stage, and he was more prepared than his great antagonist, Sir Wilfrid Laurier, and most other Canadians to confront those problems directly. While lacking the sophisticated intelligence of Woodrow Wilson, the political shrewdness of Lloyd George, and the personal dynamism of Lenin, Borden exceeded these contemporaries in patience, common sense and decency. Although a limited man, Borden knew his limitations and his nation's as well. He feared extremes in an age of immoderation, and he brought calmness,

OPPOSITE
The statue of Sir Robert Borden by Frances Loring on Parliament Hill, Ottawa.
Albert Gérin-Lajoie,
Parks Canada.

common sense and a commitment to rationality to a fanatic period. Lloyd George, Wilson, and Lenin were undoubtedly greater men, but the costs of their leadership to their nations were much more than the cost of Borden's leadership to Canada. Borden made many mistakes but he always tried to move Canada cautiously forward. Never could it be said of Borden as it was of Mackenzie King that he led us back to where we had been before. To many of his contemporaries, even to his friends, Borden seemed a plodding leader in an exciting age. But in our own age when easy solutions to civilization's discontents continue to be elusive and when reflection, patience and decency are more valued, one can better understand Robert Borden and commend his particular style.

OPPOSITE
Sir Robert Borden with his grandnephew and namesake, Robert Laird Borden, son of Henry Borden.

9
Aftermath

BORDEN'S RESOLVE to abandon politics and public life was short-lived. Within a few months of his retirement, he was preparing lectures for delivery at the University of Toronto. These lectures, thoughtful and perceptive addresses, later published as *Canadian Constitutional Studies*, testify to his continuing belief in the importance of Imperial reform and also to his own intellectual development. By 1921 he had sufficiently recovered his health to become a member of the British delegation to the Washington Conference on Naval Disarmament. Since he believed so devoutly in both an adequate voice in Imperial affairs and Anglo-American concord, his eagerness to accept this task can be easily understood. In 1922, Borden also acted for Britain in a Peruvian-British arbitration. Naturally, he continued to show an interest in and support for the League of Nations in whose foundation he had played a small role. He was a founding member of the League of Nations Society in Canada, and gave frequent speeches stressing the importance of the League and deploring all tendencies that might lead towards international anarchy. It pleased Borden immensely that within Canada and beyond, his credentials in international affairs were unquestioned.

Borden's interest in domestic politics recovered more slowly. After July 1920, he advised Meighen on political affairs, but the advice was neither so full nor so frequent as that advice he had received himself from Sir Charles Tupper after 1901. There was a good reason for this: Borden was not pleased by Canadian and Conservative political developments. Meighen had not been his first choice for the position of Conservative leader, but after he was chosen, Borden thought that Meighen's "fine qualities" would "more and more impress

themselves upon the country as he proceeds with his task."
He gradually lost this belief as political misfortune haunted
Arthur Meighen's career. The electoral disaster of 1921 began
the disillusionment: the Conservatives won only fifty seats and
became the third party in the House of Commons behind the
Progressives. In Borden's view, Meighen's problem was his
public personality. Borden confidentially advised Lord Beaverbrook before the 1925 election that "if the Conservatives did
not win the . . . election, the result would be, in no small measure, due to Mr. Meighen's unwisdom in the use of his remarkable intellectual gifts (especially his great debating
power)." Meighen, he argued, "does more harm than good
by violent attack and bitter sarcasm." In fact, the Conservatives did win the most seats in 1925, but they did not gain a
majority or the reins of government. The result of this deadlock was one of Canada's strangest political dramas performed
under the direction of Mackenzie King.

Borden had never particularly liked King; King's performance in 1925 and 1926 convinced Borden that he was
dishonest. King's confrontation with Borden's friend, Lord
Byng, and his subsequent appeal to the people aroused
Borden's latent political instincts. As a constitutional specialist,
he privately and publicly took issue with King's constitutional
arguments and supported Meighen and Lord Byng, but to no
avail. Because the stakes seemed so high, the Liberal victory
was particularly distressing to Borden. For him, the so-called
King-Byng affair established King's irresponsibility in imperial
affairs beyond the shadow of a reasonable doubt. King had
treated the imperial constitution as a political plaything; he
had mouthed the language of autonomy but he understood
neither the meaning of autonomy nor the responsibilities that
it must bring.

The disappointment of 1926 halted the rise of Borden's
spirits during the 1920s only temporarily. Throughout the
"twenties" Borden and his nation regained the confidence
lost in the previous decade. Externally, the Kellogg-Briand
pact offered the hope that war would never again occur.
Internally, prosperity prevailed, and new industries, resources
and roads pointed towards a golden future for Canada. In
1927, Canadians joyously hailed Confederation's sixtieth year,
confident that Confederation would endure. They had not
been so joyous on the occasion of the nation's golden anniver-
sary in 1917. Borden benefited from the shortness of popular
memory; more and more he was hailed as an elder statesman,

one whose wisdom and experience were a national treasure.* The 1927 Conservative Convention feted him, saluting accomplishments which not even he himself remembered. Borden was naturally delighted with the praise; he was not so pleased, however, with the Convention's choice for leader, R. B. Bennett. Bennett had been a most difficult member of the Conservative caucus; indeed, at one point Borden even questioned his sanity. After he left politics in 1917, Bennett became one of Borden's strongest critics within the Conservative Party. Borden had not forgotten this and he viewed Bennett's progress in politics with some suspicion and maintained distance in their personal relationship. There was some consolation in the choice however, since Borden's cool feelings towards Bennett made his stance as an elder statesman above politics easier to maintain.

For Borden, these autumn years were perhaps the best of all. He felt no pressure to conform, retaining his stiff Edwardian collars and refusing to learn to drive. He now had time for his beloved wild garden, his favourite Latin authors, and for old friendships strained by political passions or neglected because of overwork. There was material reward too as Borden's own fortune grew with the stock market's continuous rise. The progress of his nephew and protégé Henry may have pleased the childless Robert and Laura Borden most of all. Henry had become a Rhodes Scholar, and all indications suggested a brilliant career in law or business for the young man.† The year 1928 brought a special honour: Oxford University asked Borden, who had never attended a university, to deliver the Rhodes Memorial Lectures. Here was a welcome opportunity to reflect on the Commonwealth's growth and his own contribution to it. The lectures, which were published as *Canada and the Commonwealth*, show that the seventy-four-year-old Borden retained a surprisingly alert and informed mind. His mood is mellower than it was in Toronto in 1921, and he is more satisfied with his own work and its outcome. The tone of the lectures betrays the brightness of the age. Unfortunately, this portrait of contentment

OPPOSITE
All Saints' Church, Ottawa, draped for the State Funeral of Borden. *Public Archives Canada, C-74135.*

---

*A 1927 contest carried out by *Maclean's* ranked Borden as the third "greatest living Canadian." Two scientists, Frederick Banting and Charles Saunders, took the first two places.

†The promise was amply fulfilled. Henry became a prominent lawyer, businessman and public servant. He also edited his uncle's memoirs and his "Letters to Limbo."

and confidence in the future was soon to be shattered by worldwide depression in the 1930s.

The depression shocked Borden as it did the world; his own fortune of over a million dollars was cut in half. Even more disturbing to him was the irrationality in Canada and in the world that accompanied the economic debacle. It seemed that the madness of 1919 had returned with an uglier face, as both citizens and states brazenly shunned their responsibilities. Complete anarchy was inevitable in such circumstances. The Bennett government which was elected in 1930 attracted Borden's initial support, but, as time passed, he found the Prime Minister's performance puzzling and unsatisfactory. But Borden reserved his real contempt for the demagogues of the 1930s — Aberhart, Hepburn, Duplessis, Hitler, Stalin and Mussolini. Lacking a shred of common decency, these demagogues pandered to humanity's basest traits. What Borden said of Hepburn he thought of the others: "He is wholly lacking in a sense of the dignity of his office. In manners he is a boor, in vindictiveness a savage, and in veracity an Ananias." A world that had such leaders faced a bleak future. The failure of the League of Nations to halt the brutal attacks on Ethiopia and China convinced Borden that dark clouds enshrouded humanity's future path:

> In this turmoil of fear and hatred, of distrust, envy, jealousy and suspicion, of antagonistic nationalism, of supreme reliance on sheer force and violence, one may wonder whether what we call our civilization is destined or indeed has the right to survive.

Borden would not learn the answer to this question.

On June 10, 1937, Robert Borden died in his eighty-third year. He did not live to see the shambles of his work of 1919 and the return of Canadian troops to Europe. We do know what he would have thought of those events: humanity had evaded its collective responsibility and had to pay the price. In his final years, Borden was not a sanguine man, but he did possess internal peace and a definite sense of value that so many at the time lacked. Six months before his death, he had written of the Duke of Windsor, formerly King Edward VIII: "Let us hope that he will find in this marriage some compensation for his tragic failure to place above a foolish obsession the duty and the service that he owed to his race and its traditions and especially to the Empire's nations."

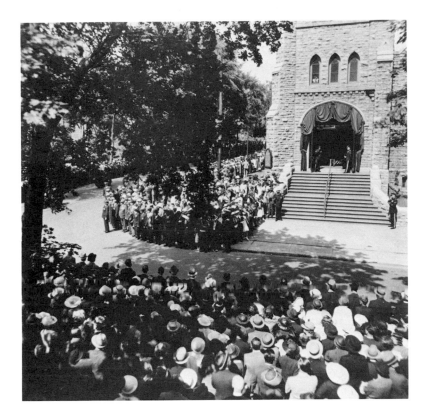

The large crowd that gathered at All Saints' Church, in Ottawa, at the time of his funeral, showed that although long in retirement, Borden was far from being a forgotten man.
Public Archives Canada, C-74134.

Robert Borden died knowing that whatever he had done, he had remained true to the duty and service that he owed his nation and his fellow human beings. For many world leaders, that knowledge would be meagre reward, but for Robert Borden, it was almost enough. That was the mark of the man.

Bibliographic Essay

Robert Borden is one of only four Canadian Prime Ministers who has written his autobiography – the others are Tupper, Pearson and Diefenbaker. Borden's two volume memoirs— *Robert Laird Borden: His Memoirs*, ed. Henry Borden (Toronto, Macmillan, 1938) — contain much detail on Borden and his times, but unfortunately, some important events are described too briefly and Borden is extremely guarded when commenting on individuals. He is more candid, however, in *Letters to Limbo*, ed. Henry Borden (Toronto, University of Toronto Press, 1971). The best of these "letters" written during the 1930s are reflective soliloquies which reveal Borden's personality better than any other published source. The first volume of the official biography by R. C. Brown has recently been published. *Robert Laird Borden: A Biography, Volume 1, 1854-1914* (Toronto, Macmillan, 1975) is indispensable to students of Borden's career. Brown's interesting approach to his subject may also be seen in his "The Political Ideas of Robert Borden," in *Les idées politiques des premiers ministres*, ed. M. Hamelin (Ottawa, University of Ottawa Press, 1969); and more fully in R. C. Brown and Ramsay Cook, *Canada, 1896-1921: A Nation Transformed* (Toronto, McClelland and Stewart, 1974).

A Nation Transformed is also the best survey of the first two decades of this century in Canada. Several recent monographs as well as numerous unpublished works provided the detailed research which permitted Brown and Cook to produce their masterly synthesis. Notable among the more specialized studies of the period are: Carl Berger, *The Sense of Power: Studies in the Ideas of Canadian Imperialism* (Toronto, University of Toronto Press, 1970), a seminal work on the imperialist movement in English Canada; Richard

Allen, *The Social Passion: Religion and Social Reform in Canada, 1914-1928* (Toronto, University of Toronto Press, 1971), a history of the Social Gospel movement in Canada; Michael Bliss, *A Living Profit: Studies in the Social History of Canadian Business, 1883-1911* (Toronto, McClelland and Stewart, 1974), a "social history" of Canadian business; Terry Copp, *The Anatomy of Poverty: The Conditions of the Working Class in Montreal, 1897-1929* (Toronto, McClelland and Stewart, 1974), which offers a glimpse of working class Montreal at the turn of the century; H. V. Nelles, *The Politics of Development: Forests, Mines and Hydro-electric Power in Ontario* (Toronto, Macmillan, 1974), an examination of the relationship between politicians and resource developers in Ontario; and Joseph Levitt, *Henri Bourassa and the Golden Calf: The Social Program of the Nationalists of Quebec 1900-1914* (Ottawa, University of Ottawa Press, 1969).

Several of Borden's colleagues and contemporaries are the subjects of biographies. The first volume of Roger Graham's biography of Arthur Meighen, *The Door of Opportunity* (Toronto, Clarke, Irwin, 1960) provides much information on the Borden administration. Margaret E. Prang's *N. W. Rowell: Ontario Nationalist* (Toronto, University of Toronto Press, 1975) is especially good on Rowell's important work in the Union Government. W. S. Wallace's biography of Sir George Foster (Toronto, Macmillan, 1933) is dated, but it does contain some interesting excerpts from Foster's diary. Scott and Astrid Young's *Silent Frank Cochrane* (Toronto, Macmillan, 1973) is highly readable but not always reliable. Ramsay Cook's *The Politics of John W. Dafoe and the Free Press* (Toronto, University of Toronto Press, 1963) describes one of Borden's early antagonists who later became an ally and friend. A. H. U. Colquhoun's biography of Sir John Willison, *Press, Politics and People* (Toronto, Macmillan, 1935) studies another Liberal journalist who underwent a similar experience. Finally, any serious student of the period must read the second volume of O. D. Skelton's *The Life and Letters of Sir Wilfrid Laurier* (Toronto, Oxford, 1921) and J. W. Dafoe's *Clifford Sifton in Relation to His Times* (Toronto, Macmillan, 1931). Both are well written, highly perceptive biographies which evoke the atmosphere of the period while sketching two of its most important personalities.

Until recently, the European battleground attracted more attention than the domestic events of the war years. The bibliography on the war is too vast to cite here, but two works stand out: G. W. L. Nicholson, *The Canadian Expeditionary Force 1914-1919* (Ottawa, Dept. of National Defence, 1962) and John Swettenham, *To Seize the Victory* (Toronto, McGraw-Hill, 1965). On the controversial question of conscription, see A. C. Willms, "Conscription, A Brief for the Defence," *Canadian Historical Review*, XXXVII (Dec. 1956); W. R. Young, "Conscription, Rural Depopulation and the Farmers of Ontario, 1917-1919," *Canadian Historical Review*, LIII (Sept. 1972), 289-320; and Elizabeth Armstrong, *The Crisis of Quebec*, 1914-1918 (Toronto, McClelland and Stewart, 1974). Surprisingly, there is no full study of Canada's changing international role during and after the war. Among the many fine articles on the subject are R. C. Brown, "Sir Robert Borden, the Great War and Anglo-Canadian Relations" in John Moir, ed., *Character and Circumstance: Essays in Honour of D. G. Creighton* (Toronto, Macmillan, 1970), 201-224; and R. S. Bothwell, "Canadian Representation at Washington: A Study in Colonial Responsibility," *Canadian Historical Review*, LIII (June, 1972), 125-148.

A Borden supporter, Stephen Leacock, dominated Canadian literature during Borden's tenure as Prime Minister. Several of his best works — *Nonsense Novels* (1911), *Sunshine Sketches of a Little Town* (1912), *Arcadian Adventure with the Idle Rich* (1914) and *Moonbeams from the Larger Lunacy* (1915) — are widely available in paperback reprints. The best known novel of the period is the Frenchman Louis Hémon's *Maria Chapdelaine* (1916), a novel about rural life in Quebec. By contrast, the troubled city of Winnipeg, during the strike, is the setting of Douglas Durkin's *The Magpie* (1923), perhaps the best fictional portrait of Canada's post-war turmoil. The best-selling novelist prior to and during the war was Ralph Connor (Rev. Charles Gordon). Connor's *The Major* (1917) is worth reading as an example of how Canadian literature became propaganda during the war years. That some Canadian artists also served the state is revealed in A. Y. Jackson's *A Painter's Country* (Toronto, Clarke, Irwin, 1976), a charming autobiography which also discusses the new trends in Canadian painting which culminated in the 1920s in the celebrated Group of Seven. Suffragette Nellie McClung's 1915 book, *In Times Like These*, discusses the large impact of the war on women and women on the war.

Index